SHAPING THE
CONGREGATION

Into Our Third Century Series

SHAPING THE CONGREGATION

ROBERT L. WILSON

Ezra Earl Jones, Editor

ABINGDON   Nashville

SHAPING THE CONGREGATION

Library of Congress Cataloging in Publication Data

WILSON, ROBERT LEROY, 1925-
  Shaping the congregation.
  Includes bibliographical references.
  (Into our third century)
  1. Church. 2. Sociology, Christian (Methodist)
I. Title. II. Series.
BX8331.2.W54   287'.6   80-22228

ISBN 0-687-38334-X

MANUFACTURED BY THE PARTHENON PRESS AT
NASHVILLE, TENNESSEE, UNITED STATES OF AMERICA

TO

Rockwell C. Smith

**from whom
I learned much about
local churches**

Contents

Foreword

In 1984 United Methodism will observe the two hundredth anniversary of the Christmas Conference of 1784—the date most often regarded as the beginning of the Methodist movement in the United States. We shall pause to remember how the Wesleyan vision of holy love and active piety spread like an unquenchable flame as the United States expanded from coast to coast; how people of all races, cultures, and classes rallied to a gospel offering salvation and demanding good works as the fruit of Christian faith in God.

But we shall do more. Our bicentennial is also a time to soberly anticipate the future, to take stock of ourselves as we move into our third century. Our inheritance is rich in faith and works. It nourishes us but our tasks are now, and tomorrow. The United Methodist Church is large (9.6 million members in the United States), still highly visible and active, but some indicators of our future prospects are disturbing. We shall reflect on and discuss these concerns as United Methodists until we once again catch a vision of ministry and service that is worthy of our past, builds upon our present, and thrusts us again into the mainstream of human life with the message of God's redeeming love.

You, a United Methodist lay member or pastor, and your congregation have a vital role in both the celebration and the search. It is the people in the pews and pulpits of United Methodism who must reestablish their identity and purpose through discussion on who we are as United Methodists, what they wish to accomplish, and how they will pursue their goals in the years ahead.

The *Into Our Third Century* Series, initiated by the General Council on Ministries with the encouragement of the Council of Bishops, is intended to support these efforts. It is an extensive study of selected issues of fundamental ministry and organizational concern to the denomination and a study of the environment in which United Methodism in the United States serves. Over a four-year period, beginning in 1980, eighteen separate volumes are being released for your use. The present book *Shaping the Congregation* is the fifth volume in the series. Subsequent volumes will deal with outreach ministry (mission, evangelism, and social witness), social movements and issues, church leadership and management, nonparish institutions (for example, colleges, hospitals, homes, community centers), ecumenical relationships, ethnic minority constituencies, understanding faith (the role of theology), professional ministry, the role of general agencies, financial support patterns, and polity (the philosophy and form of church government and the organization).

The General Council on Ministries commends to you this volume by Robert L. Wilson. It is a book about the local church. It is intended to assist pastors and laity to understand the nature of the congregation as a social institution, among other social institutions, in the community where it is located and which it serves.

Did you ever wonder why United Methodist churches are so much alike in some ways, yet so different in others? Or how and why they differ from churches of other denominations? Dr. Wilson analyzes the forces and factors that have made United Methodist congregations unique, that contributed to their rapid growth in frontier America, and that may be related to the failure of the denomination to keep pace with population growth in the United States in recent years.

From a study by Wilson and a panel of colleagues at Duke University and elsewhere, we discover that the United Methodist local church is an institution established, organized, and governed by a denominational system that evolved from a reform movement initiated by Wesley. It is distinctive in Western church history. It just may have been the best system of starting churches, deploying pastors, reaching the lost, and attacking social ills in nineteenth century America. But Wilson raises questions about its viability today and offers suggestions for change.

You will find your local church in this book. You will come to see the theological, historical, and social forces that have made the congregation what it is and are helping to account for its present internal dynamics. We believe that this understanding will assist you in finding a direction for the congregation in the future as social realities change and the church either changes too or declines. Share your reflections within your own congregation, with other Christians, and with district, conference, and general church leaders. Your response will also be welcomed by the members and staff of the Council.

Norman E. Dewire
General Secretary

Ezra Earl Jones
Editor

The General Council on Ministries
601 West Riverview Avenue
Dayton, Ohio 45406

January, 1981

Introduction

In an adult church school class at the Asbury United Methodist Church, Sarah, one of the longtime saints of the congregation, made the comment, "It just doesn't seem right that there are so many churches in this town. All of us worship the same God. Why can't we be together?" A similar thought has probably crossed the minds of most church members, particularly as they contemplate the cost of a new roof for the educational building, the need to raise the pastor's salary, or the slim attendance on a rainy Sunday morning.

While on vacation George and Ann worshiped at a church of a denomination different from the one to which they belong. After the service George observed, "I could never join that church. The informality didn't appeal to me, and I didn't like the music. The whole atmosphere seemed to lack dignity."

As these persons noted, local chuches are not alike. They differ in a variety of ways, ranging from the style of worship to the kinds of activities that the members find acceptable and meaningful. While significant differences between congregations are found between those of different denominations, considerable variations can be noted even among churches of the same denomination. The local churches and the differences between them are

13

the result of two factors: the theological beliefs to which the members subscribe and the social forces within the congregation and the larger community in which it is located. The interaction of the theological assumptions and the social forces determines what a particular local church is and does.

This book will consider the theological and social factors that influence the life of the local church. The major focus will be the social forces that affect the local church. Areas to be considered will include the impact of the larger community, the congregation as a social group, the relationship of the clergy and laity, and the relationship of the congregation to other local churches and to the denomination.

While the congregations of the various Protestant churches have many common characteristics, the different traditions, forms of government, and theological assumptions give some degree of uniqueness to each. This book will focus on those forces that shape United Methodist local churches.

The purpose of this book is to help Christian people better understand how the social forces within the community, the congregation, and the denomination influence the nature and the functioning of the local church. We hope this understanding will help them make their congregation more effective in its task of witnessing to the faith, providing a supportive fellowship, and serving the larger community.

As The United Methodist Church will soon enter its third century, it finds itself in a period of severe institutional crisis. In the decade following the Methodist and Evangelical United Brethren merger, 1969–78, the denomination declined by 11 percent. This represents a loss of 1,217,977 members. During this period the number of organized local churches decreased by over 2,068, or 5 percent.

The seriousness of this situation can be dramatized by noting that every week during that entire decade The United Methodist Church lost an average of 2,342 members and closed four local churches. To put it another way, if the denomination continues to lose members at the same rate, it will not be around to begin its fourth century; it will have gone out of existence early in the last quarter of its third century.

The material that follows will not provide easy anwers to the complex question of how to reverse the downward membership trend. But we hope it will help United Methodist people better understand the local church and contribute to their finding ways of making it more effective. This is the first step in reversing the recent trends.

This book is one of several being sponsored by the General Council on Ministries of The United Methodist Church to commemorate the denomination's bicentennial. The author is indebted to the General Council on Ministries and to Ezra Earl Jones, director of the Third Century Project, for support of this research. A particular word of appreciation goes to present and former colleagues who served as members on an Advisory Committee to the project, prepared background papers, or gave valuable counsel: Dennis M. Campbell, Paula E. Gilbert, Lawrence E. Johnson, Paul A. Mickey, Alan K. Waltz, and William H. Willimon. Finally, special thanks goes to Mrs. Anne Daniels, secretary in the Ormond Center, who typed the manuscript.

As The United Methodist Church enters its third century, its task will certainly be as difficult as in the past.

It is the hope of all who had a part in this project that this book will help United Methodist people better understand their church and thus enable them to make it more effective in witnessing to the faith and building Christian community.

PART I

Factors Which Form
United Methodist
Congregations

CHAPTER 1

Theological Factors

While all churches share a common origin and heritage, each denomination subscribes to theological assumptions to which it gives special emphasis. These contribute to the uniqueness of the denomination and its local churches. This chapter will examine those aspects of United Methodist theology that have influenced the organization and functioning of the local church. It will consider the beginnings of United Methodism in the Anglican tradition, the changes brought about by the transition to America, and finally some of the current theological understandings that are having an impact on the congregation.[1]

The Background

Methodism emerged out of Anglicanism and yet incorporated some free church tendencies. The Anglican Church owes its beginning less to theological reasons than do the other great Protestant movements, Lutheranism and Calvinism. In England the Reformation was more an act of state and less a religious reform than on the continent. It first differed from Roman Catholicism mainly in regard to the role of the bishop of Rome. In Anglicanism the monarch became head of the church;

Roman Catholicism insisted on the supremacy of the pope.

There are several characteristics of the Church of England that are of special significance for understanding Methodism. First, the Anglican Church retained the threefold order of ministry that had emerged very early in the Christian church. This threefold ministry includes deacons, presbyters, and bishops. Apostolic succession, which means that the authority of the churches is preserved by a direct succession from the earliest apostles through the imposition of the hands of a bishop at ordination, was emphasized.

Second, Anglicanism retained the catholic emphasis on the liturgical and sacramental life of the church. Principal attention was given to the sacraments of Holy Communion and baptism although some ambiguity was permitted about the other five sacraments of confirmation, ordination, holy matrimony, penitence, and unction. Anglican theology has not deviated in its insistence on the centrality of sacramental worship.

Third, Anglican theology retained the catholic understanding of the church as the mediator of God's grace to men and women in the world. The authority of the church in matters of faith and practice is therefore not subject to the individual claims of Christian believers. Moreover, the church is the Body of Christ in the world through which persons come to faith in God, in Jesus Christ and to salvation.

Fourth, Anglicanism was the product of a compromise both theologically and politically. While it required conformity, it also retained the possibility of wide latitude within the guidelines of the historic creeds and Articles of Religion. *The Book of Common Prayer* was to be the guide to faith and practice and the service contained therein was to be used. But the paragraphs of the Articles of Religion to be emphasized were left largely to the discretion of individual clergy. The Church of England permitted diversity within conformity. The limits of faith and practice were clear, but a variety of opinion and practice was tolerated.

Fifth, the Anglican Church retained the catholic idea that a state needed to have one official state church. This meant that Anglicanism considered itself to be the church for the Christians in England. Church and State were combined on the theory that the unity of the state depended on shared religious practices. Persons who rejected the state church were designated dissenters.

Methodism developed within the Anglican Church. The United Methodist understanding of the church has been shaped by this Anglican heritage. Therefore, United Methodism's character is different from that of other Protestant groups on the continent, a difference that has resulted in a distinctive combination of catholic and evangelical theology. Wesley's theology of the church was rooted in the Anglican heritage. He never left the Church of England but regarded Methodism as a reform movement within that church. It was his hope that the Church of England would welcome the evangelical revival as an opportunity for new vitality and a way to minister to increased numbers of people. Wesley vehemently objected to the suggestion that Methodists were dissenters and urged regular attendance at the services of the Anglican Church. The gradual movement of Methodism away from the Church of England during Wesley's life and its eventual split with that church after his death was never Wesley's intention.

John Wesley never wrote a systematic theological statement about the church and one must study his sermons and facts to understand his viewpoint. In writing about the church he cited the nineteenth article of the Thirty-nine Articles of Religion of the Church of England:

> The visible Church of Christ is a congregation of faithful men, in the which the pure Word of God is preached, and the Sacraments be duly ministered according to Christ's ordinance, in all those things that of necessity are requisite to the same.
>
> As the Church of Jerusalem, Alexandria, and Antioch, have erred; so also the Church of Rome hath erred, not only in their living and manner of Ceremonies, but also in matters of Faith.

Wesley accepted this definition of the church without question and interpreted it in a way to suggest that a universal church is comprised of numerous churches. He was unwilling to make stringent judgments about particular expressions of the Christian faith and community. There is a spirit of inclusiveness in Wesley's understanding of the church, which is consistent with his theological conviction regarding people's capacity and freedom to respond to God. In his sermon, "Of the Church," Wesley interpreted Ephesians 4:1-6 as follows:

> Here, then, is a clear unexceptionable answer to that question, "What is the Church?" The catholic or universal Church is all the persons in the universe whom God hath so called out of the world as to entitle them to the preceding character—as to be "one body," united by "one Spirit," having "one faith, one hope, one baptism; one God and Father of all, who is above all, and through all, and in them all."[2]

In Wesley's view the church included the possibility of small groups of faithful believers coming together within the church for study, worship, and discipline. The church was to be inclusive rather than exclusive. It was to be evangelical. Indeed, it was this evangelical emphasis that Wesley considered to be missing from eighteenth-century Anglicanism.

Wesley believed that small groups were the key to Christian life. Unsatisfied with what he perceived to be the lack of community in the Church of England, Wesley insisted that the Methodist people be members of small groups. He established band societies and classes in which the people learned, shared, prayed, and reexamined their Christian practices. The development of these groups and the constant nurturing of them by Methodist leaders was the fundamental aspect of Wesley's program. They were the foundation upon which Methodism grew. Wesley's organizational genius gave birth to a pattern that was to become the hallmark of early Methodism. Congregations of believers were not alone but part of a connection in which they were bound together. Wesley advanced the idea of connectionalism to a point where it became perhaps his greatest contribution to church polity.

Wesley sought to hold the catholic and evangelical emphases in church theology together. During his lifetime, however, serious strains developed between Anglicanism and Methodism. The bishops and the vast majority of the clergy opposed the new movement. Methodists on the other hand saw little reason to participate in the parish churches, despite Wesley's insistence that they do so. He continued to urge regular attendance at church, frequent reception of the Holy Communion, and no Methodist society meeting during regular church hours. However, the rapid growth of Methodism soon made it impossible for it to remain a movement within Anglicanism.

Consideration of early Methodist theology of the

church must include John Wesley's controversial ordinations. These became an issue because of a serious problem among the church leaders in America. The preachers there were not ordained and could not celebrate the sacraments. There had been few Anglican clergy in the colonies and many of them left during the Revolutionary War. There was no Anglican bishop in North America. Wesley was concerned that his people were being deprived of the sacraments. The Bishop of London, in whose diocese America was, would take no steps to remedy the situation despite Wesley's appeals. Convinced that some action was necessary, Wesley took the unprecedented step of ordaining two men for the ministry and consecrating the third as a "superintendent." On September 1, 1784, Wesley ordained Richard Whatcoat and Thomas Vasey deacons. The next day he ordained them presbyters and consecrated the Reverend Thomas Coke, an episcopally ordained clergyman of the Anglican Church, superintendent.

By assuming the authority to ordain, Wesley was breaking church law and discipline. His justification was both practical and theoretical. The practical problem was clear; there was a need for ordained clergy among the Methodist people in America. Wesley believed that the practical needs of evangelical Christianity had to be met.

Wesley also struggled to satisfy himself that his actions were theologically sound. He did not challenge the need for church order or the historic idea of apostolic succession. It was his conviction that a bishop is a presbyter who has been consecrated to serve the church in a special way. Presbyters therefore might exercise the role of *episkopoi in extremis.* The need of American Methodists to receive Holy Communion was considered by Wesley an extreme case. Wesley found precedent in the Church of Alexandria during the first three centuries of the Christian era where presbyters were elected and ordained their bishops without the external imposition of hands. While the argument may be subtle, the point is that Wesley is consistent in his effort to be both catholic and evangelical, both theologically careful and practically resourceful. Wesley was technically in violation of church law, but his theology of the church included the possibility of dramatic and unconventional acts to enhance the evangelical mission.

Transition to America

The first Methodist societies in America were founded by laymen in New York and Baltimore in 1768. Methodist identity before the Revolution was ambiguous due to the precarious relationship with the Church of England. Methodism was identified with that church and yet it was distinct and different. The difference increased during the Revolutionary War when most Anglican clergy left the colonies. At the close of the war Wesley took his unprecedented step of ordaining men for service in America. At the Christmas Conference held in Baltimore on December 24, 1784, the Methodist Episcopal Church was formed. Francis Asbury who had arrived in America as a young preacher in 1771 had been nominated by Wesley to become superintendent at the Baltimore Conference. However, Asbury insisted on election by the sixty preachers present before he would be ordained by Coke. Asbury and Coke, to Wesley's horror, adopted the title "bishop." After the Baltimore Conference, the Methodist Episcopal Church in America became an independent denomination, not simply an extension of British Methodism.

Asbury was a brilliant organizer who was able to lead the new church during a period of remarkable growth.

He was not a theologian; the frontier setting was not conducive to scholarly theological reflection. Nevertheless, patterns and procedures established during this early period have shaped the Methodist Church.

First, the Methodist Church chose to become an episcopal church. The meaning of the episcopal office in Methodism has been the subject of much study and debate. The fact is, however, that early Methodists gave the office great authority and significance. They firmly rejected Presbyterian and Congregational polity. The threefold historical ministry was preserved. By its choice of an episcopal structure, American Methodism sought to understand itself as a participant in the historical holy catholic church. The theological implications of this decision have affected all aspects of church life, including the structure and organization of the local church.

Second, the Methodist Episcopal Church understood its ministers as being itinerant members of the Annual Conference and not just leaders of a local congregation. The Methodist minister was and continues to be ordained by a bishop. The Annual Conference establishes standards and rules for candidates for ministerial orders. The theological significance of this is that God's call to the ministry is not to a local church but to the universal church. Accountability in ministry is therefore not only to the local congregation but also to the church as a whole. Ministers are not creatures of a local church; they are assigned to the pastorate of the church according to ability and need. Itineracy is a system designed to benefit the entire church. Methodism sought to witness to the fact that the church is not confined to a local manifestation of Christian community.

Third, the Methodist Episcopal Church chose to understand the local congregation as part of a connectional church. The local congregation is not independent and it is not free to act on its own. This symbolizes the unity of the church in Christ and is intended to dispel an overemphasis on localism. The connectionalism of the Christian church was one of Wesley's major theological convictions.

Fourth, Methodism chose to structure itself in a manner that provided for flexibilty in carrying out its mission. The early organization of the church was uniquely suited to the needs of the developing country and people living on the American frontier. The Annual Conferences and the episcopal leadership could provide ministry even in the most remote parts of the nation. Methodism's rapid growth in the early nineteenth century was a result of this flexibility.

Fifth, the Methodist Episcopal Church perceived its mission to be the spreading of evangelical holiness to as many persons as possible. The church was to minister not only to needs of its members but also to those outside the church.

Sixth, Methodism understood itself to have a social responsibility. Personal holiness was not enough; there was concern for society and the creation of a social order consistent with the will of God. Methodism became highly involved in the reform movements in the early nineteenth century, a practice that has continued. The church saw no division between personal holiness and social commitment. In fact, Methodism demanded that high standards of personal moral conviction be translated into public life.

These six points reflect the close relationship between polity and theology in early American Methodism. While Methodism in the United States was acquired through Wesley, the American setting necessitated some theological and polity accommodations. The church in this country came to give less attention to liturgy and the sacraments than Wesley had recommended. This was no less for theological than for practical reasons. The frontier setting of the small congregations did not lend itself to formal liturgical worship; ordained ministers itinerated over large circuits so that the services were often led by unordained persons who were unable to celebrate the sacraments.

Wesley's determination to hold together catholic and Anglican understandings of the nature and purpose of the church was continued in America. The close relationship between the theology and polity was enhanced as adjustments were made to accommodate to the particular needs of the developing denomination. The impact of these developments for the local churches was significant. No congregation was left without close and constant pastoral oversight. Even Bishop Francis Asbury made regular visits to local Methodist churches. His circuit was the entire denomination and he covered it once a year. Congregations were founded as new settlements were established. The polity served the local church as it advanced the evangelical mission of the entire church.

While early American Methodists may not have produced learned theologies, practical theology informed the church. A mixture of catholic and evangelical understandings was constantly present. The catholic emphases prescribed order, a doctrine of ministry and episcopal structure, and a continuity with the historic apostolic church. The evangelical emphases required that the particular setting of ministry be taken seriously, that the practical needs of the church not be lost in the tradition, and that the aggressive communication of the gospel be central to the church's mission.

United Methodist Theology of the Church

The early American Methodist Episcopal Church was built upon Wesley's foundation, but it often significantly modified Wesley's ideas. As the denomination developed, it went through a number of structural and organizational changes; some groups broke away while others joined. Through all these organizational changes, a consistent theology of the church is evident. The United Methodist Church, founded in 1968 as the result of the merger of The Methodist Church and The Evangelical United Brethren Church, is the chief inheritor of the theological tradition of American Methodism. The Preamble to the Constitution of the Church states:

> The Church is a community of all true believers under the Lordship of Christ. It is the redeemed and redeeming fellowship in which the Word of God is preached by persons divinely called, and the Sacraments are duly administered according to Christ's own appointment. Under the discipline of the Holy Spirit the Church seeks to provide for the maintenance of worship, the edification of believers, and the redemption of the world.
>
> The Church of Jesus Christ exists in and for the world, and its very dividedness is a hindrance to its mission in that world.[3]

This statement is a summary of several Methodist foundational affirmations about the church including: Article XIII of the Articles of Religion of The Methodist Church prepared by John Wesley in 1784; Article V of the Confession of Faith of The Evangelical United Brethren Church; Paragraphs 201, 202, and 203 of *The Book of Discipline of The United Methodist Church* dealing with the local church; and the affirmation that is read by

the minister at the beginning of the service of Confirmation and Reception into the Church:

> Dearly beloved, the Church is of God, and will be preserved
> to the end of time, for the conduct of worship and the due
> administration of his Word and Sacraments, the mainte-
> nance of Christian fellowship and discipline, the edification
> of believers, and the conversion of the world. All, of every age
> and station, stand in need of the means of grace which it
> alone supplies.[4]

These foundational documents become important
only when it is seen how they provide the basis for a
particular polity. United Methodist theology of the
church is manifest in United Methodism's unique
structure and organization. The major decisions made by
the early American Methodists were consistent with the
theological assumptions that informed Methodism from
its beginnings. Those decisions about ministry, connection, mission, emphasis on preaching, and the importance of standards of personal conduct were theological
decisions as well as practical decisions. They identified
Methodism with certain distinctive traditions within
Christianity, and they set Methodism apart from other
theological traditions.

The United Methodist Church is inclusive and theologically diverse. This is not because it lacks theology, but
because the United Methodist theology of the church is
reluctant to make narrow and absolute statements about
dogma. It is difficult, indeed, to determine precisely what
it means to speak of "Methodist theology." This is
because John Wesley, offering his own interpretation of
catholic teaching about theological methodology, prescribed a fourfold set of norms by which Christian

doctrine is judged. These norms are *Scripture, tradition, reason,* and *experience.* The interaction of these guidelines is complex; Scripture is given priority, but the *Discipline* insists that ". . . all four guidelines be brought to bear upon every doctrinal consideration" (Paragraph 69).

Some people are frustrated when they realize that diversity of theological position is inevitable because the four norms can interact in a variety of ways to produce Christian theology. The strength of this tradition is its flexibility and practicality. The weakness is that it is difficult to make a firm statement of United Methodist theology. The church community for United Methodism becomes the integrating reality for theology. Diversity is tolerated as long as it is in service to the church. The limits to diversity are established in the creative setting of Christian community, which is authored and judged by the working of God's Holy Spirit.

The church is the community in which and for which theology is done. United Methodist theology works out of the four authoritative norms in the community that consciously identifies itself with the United Methodist tradition. The church is an association of men and women who choose to be part of it and who choose to be in service to the world in the name of Jesus Christ. Despite human inadequacy in theological understanding and in Christian action, the church mediates God's grace unto the world. United Methodists have been hesitant to limit God's work in the church and have thus seen the church as an inclusive community.

United Methodist theology of the church continues to seek to hold together the catholic and evangelical ideas. The emphasis on church order, participation in the holy catholic church, the ordained ministry, and sacramental life are marks of its maintenance of catholic tradition;

and its concern for personal commitment. Strict rules of personal conduct, classes, and accountability are marks of its evangelical concern. Any theological understanding of United Methodism must take note of this uniting of catholic and evangelical ideas.

CHAPTER 2

Events in United Methodism's Past

A denomination is not only shaped by its theological assumptions or belief system but by the historical context in which it was formed. The interaction of the church's theological beliefs with the social forces present in the society at critical periods determines the nature and direction of the denomination. Characteristics developed at critical periods become part of a tradition accepted as the proper way of performing the mission of the church. This common tradition is a source of pride and gives the members a sense of identity. It helps them understand the ways in which a United Methodist is different from a Baptist or a Presbyterian.

The forces that have had a determining influence in shaping United Methodism are many and complex. This chapter will highlight several that have been influential in shaping the denomination and particularly the local church.[1]

Wesley's Organizational Imprint

No individual has been more influential in shaping United Methodism than has John Wesley. His influence on United Methodist theology has been noted; his impact on the organization and functioning of the local church will now be discussed. There are five specific areas in which Wesley's influence has been particularly significant.

The first and most important is Wesley's practicality, a functional style of operation that could be termed expedient. There was in Wesley a pragmatic commonsense approach combined with the ability to recognize the general acceptability of successful experiments. When something worked, he utilized it throughout the societies. Wesley at times had difficulty breaking with traditions but, in the end, what was necessary to further the goals of faith was accepted. This approach is illustrated in Wesley's *A Plain Account of the People Called Methodists.*

> . . . they had not the least expectation, at first, of any thing like what has since followed, so they had no previous design or plan at all; but every thing arose just as the occasion offered. They saw or felt some impending or pressing evil, or some good end necessary to be pursued. And many times they fell unawares on the very thing which secured the good, or removed the evil. At other times, they consulted on the most probable means, following only common sense and the Scripture.

The second and third aspects of Wesley's institutional leadership style—organization and discipline—are a result of his functional approach. Organization in the Wesleyan heritage refers explicitly to that pattern which has become known as the connectional system. During Wesley's lifetime the connectional system developed into an interlocking network of bands, classes, societies, lay preachers, and other lay leaders, circuits, the circuit quarterly meeting, and Annual Conferences. The result was to produce a brand of church polity that was neither Presbyterian, Congregational, nor diocesan Episcopalianism although it had some elements from each. The Methodist connectional system increased organizational efficiency and enhanced group loyalty. This connectional system is still a central tenet of the denomination, although there are signs that it is weakening. The local churches no longer receive the degree of supervision that they did in the past.

For a connectional system to function, a high degree of discipline is necessary. For Wesley, spiritual discipline was an integral part of the religious life; discipline in other areas of life naturally followed. The people, and particularly the clergy, not only had to be loyal to the organization but also had to submit to the discipline of the group and the rules by which the individual and the church operated. Throughout his life Wesley stressed discipline, the following of rules and regulations. In 1743 he set forth the rules for the societies in *The Nature, Design, and General Rules of Our United Societies,* thus clarifying what was expected of Methodists.

A fourth element in Methodism, which was a result of Wesley's functional approach, was lay leadership. With the exception of a few ordained clergy, the early period was one of lay leadership and lay initiative. It was ordinary men and women who became traveling preachers, local preachers, class leaders, band leaders, and stewards. Because of their efforts the Methodist revival was carried throughout England and to the American colonies.

A final factor that helped shape the Methodist organization was Wesley's catholic spirit. This too is an extension of his functional approach. In his sermon, "Catholic Spirit,"[2] Wesley asks the famous question, "Is thine heart right, as my heart is with thy heart?" and follows it with the response, "If it be, give me thy hand." One of Wesley's recurring motifs was his stress on those essentials of the faith that bind Christians together. Thus, he could welcome the Arminian and Calvinistic wings of the revival and seek to unite their efforts, and allow some collaboration with dissenting groups as the Presbyterians, Independents, Anabaptists, and Quakers. He even sought a measure of reconciliation with Roman Catholics by arguing in an open letter that the basics of Christianity may be found in the injunction to love God and to love the neighbor. Thus a narrow doctrinal stance would not prevent Methodists from working with other groups in their task of proclaiming the gospel and striving for the common good.

A New Church in a New Nation

The fact that the Wesleyan movement in England and its beginnings in the colonies and the independence of the United States occurred at the same time had enormous significance for the development of Methodism in America. The emergence of the new nation made it inevitable that the church also would be independent. The distances across the Atlantic, the slowness of the crossing, and the sheer size of the new nation would have made administration of American Methodism from England very difficult; the independence movement made it impossible. In the wake of the Revolutionary War, a church that was not based in America would have found little favor.

John Wesley, being the pragmatist that he was, took the necessary steps for American Methodism to become an independent denomination. Writing to "Our Brethren in America," Wesley states, "They are now at full liberty simply to follow the Scriptures and the Primitive Church. And we judge it best that they should stand fast in that liberty wherewith God has so strangely made them free."[3]

From the Christmas Conference of 1784, the church began its development separate from the parent group in England. Two factors combined to greatly influence the institutional nature of American Methodism and significantly contribute to the growth of what was to become one of the major Protestant denominations in the United States.

The first factor was the centralized control, which was inherited from Wesley and carried forward by Francis Asbury and other leaders of American Methodism. The authority to send preachers was clearly that of the bishop; the members of a congregation were not permitted to call their pastor. Methodism was held together by a group of disciplined clergy who accepted the assignment and supervision of the bishop and who were responsible to one another.

Such a church organization was uniquely suited for ministry to a growing nation. Independence had opened the vast western territories and settlers were pushing westward into the piedmont, across the Appalachian Mountains, and on to seemingly endless plains. The nineteenth century was characterized by mobility and development. Trails were cut through the wilderness in time to be followed by roads and rail lines; farms were established and settlements begun. It was an unsettled period, a time of development and transition, of successes and failures, of dreams realized and unmarked graves along the trails west.

Probably no form of church organization was better suited to bringing the gospel to a mobile population than was the Methodist. The assignment of a preacher to a circuit or a territory was made by the denomination; the minister did not have to await the formation of a congregation, which would issue a call. The circuit rider, like the people he served, was mobile. He could seek out the settlements and organize the people into societies, thus providing for religious activities during the periods when he was not present.

The second factor was the establishing of Annual Conferences. The pattern tended to be for an Annual Conference to be organized between the time an area acquired territorial status and statehood. In only seven instances was a state admitted into the union before a Methodist Annual Conference was organized. The success of Methodism in this period can be noted by examining the distribution of the present members. The denomination has had great strength in rural and small town America in the Midwest and the South, the sections where Methodism was established during the first half of the nineteenth century.

The size of the United States and the broad distribution of Methodist members made it inevitable that the denomination would be organized into regional judicatories. The result has been that The United Methodist Church became and remains a confederation of Annual Conferences. The Annual Conference continues to be the basic unit, particularly for the clergy. The ministerial members of the Annual Conferences decide who shall be admitted into the ministry. The conference sets the clergy pensions and other benefits. Most clergy spend their careers serving churches in one Annual Conference. It is the Annual Conference that determines the amount of money to be paid by the local churches and decides on the programs in which congregations are expected to participate.

The tradition of centralized authority and the development of the clergy-controlled Annual Conference produced a denomination that is still dominated by the ordained clergy. There is a touch of irony in the fact that a religious movement, which in its beginning was largely led by laypersons, should develop into a denomination which, despite attempts to give greater authority to the laity, is still largely controlled by ordained ministers. The patterns firmly established in the early period are still very much a part of United Methodism as it enters its third century.

From Society to Denomination

The Methodist movement, as we have seen, began as a reform movement within the Church of England.

As a religious society and not a church, Methodism had limited aims, powers, and responsibilities. Membership in a society did not replace membership in the church. This relationship to the Anglican Church was carried to America and existed until the Christmas Conference of 1784. At that time, by the decision of the assembled preachers and with the blessing of Wesley himself, the Methodist movement in America declared its independence and established itself as the Methodist Episcopal Church. It officially became a denomination and began the process of evolution from a loose association of scattered societies to a church.

The characteristics of Methodism as a society and as a church have been presented by William Pitt MacVey in his book *The Genius of Methodism*. The societies had five characteristics, which were changed as Methodism became a church. The societies had a simple doctrinal basis; the individual could join a society and still retain membership in the church. No pretensions were made by the societies to ecclesiastical functions such as providing the sacraments. The governing power resided in John Wesley. The societies existed to perform certain spiritual functions. In contrast to the societies, the independent Methodist Episcopal Church provided a revised version of the Articles of Religion. Membership took the place of any previous church affiliation. The new organization was explicitly a church and exercised all the functions thereof. The relationship with Mr. Wesley was severed with the governing power going to the conference, whose membership consisted of the clergy.

The early Methodist societies can be perceived as a sect that gradually developed into a church. This process continued over most of the denomination's history and it is now virtually complete. The long-term effect on United Methodist congregations has been profound. The fervor of the early lay-led societies is a part of the tradition that is no longer operative, a tradition that is looked upon with some pride but not emulated. The denomination and its component congregations perceive themselves as a respected and respectable part of the society, as organizations where things are done decently and in order, an important and powerful segment of America's religious establishment.

CHAPTER 3

Social Forces

The local church is not only shaped by the theology of its adherents and its historical development, but also formed by the social forces in the community in which it is located and in the larger society. It is the interaction of the theological assumptions of a particular church and the social forces in the community that determine the nature of a congregation, the kind of people who are likely to become members, the style of worship, and the type of programs and mission which are meaningful. This chapter will focus on the social factors that help shape the local church.

The Social Function of Religion

An institution is the organization of several folkways and mores or ways of thinking, believing, and acting, into a unit, which serves a number of social functions. Five basic institutions are necessary for a society to function. These are the family and the educational, economic, political, and religious institutions. These provide for the reproduction of the race, preserving of the cultural heritage and socializing the young, securing and distributing material necessities, assuring order in the society, and giving life meaning and value.

Every society has a religion although its form and organization vary widely. Religion does four things that help maintain the dominance of group sentiment and aims over individual desires and private interests. First, it offers a system of supernatural beliefs that justify the primacy of group aims. Second, it provides through its rituals a constant renewal of the common beliefs and opportunity for commitment to them. Third, it provides a place where people who share the same beliefs can gather. Fourth, it provides a source of unlimited rewards for those who have the right beliefs and exhibit the proper conduct, and punishment for those who do not. In the Christian tradition these functions of religion have been carried out within the context of the local church. The parish church has been one of the Western society's most durable institutions, and there are no indications that it is likely to be replaced.

If we examine what goes on in local churches we can note the ways the above functions are carried out. The people are admonished to put the group and even the society ahead of their own interests, to give sacrificially of their time and their money. The pastor reminds the people that the church is the most important thing in their lives and that they should give it first priority.

The form that the worship service takes reminds the people who they are and what they believe. The sameness of liturgy is a continual reaffirmation of the group, its beliefs and goals. Conflict over changes in the ritual can be intense because discarding old and accepted rituals threatens the group's self-understanding and identity. An example of such a controversy is the one over the adoption of a new prayer book by the Episcopal Church. This was a contributing factor in a schism that resulted in the withdrawal of a number of members and churches and the formation of a new denomination.

People gather in a place, a church building, where they share common experiences. Church buildings take on a sacredness that we encounter when there is a proposal to relocate or even to rearrange the physical facilities. The physical space has symbolic meaning, which represents the shared values and even the group itself. The resistance encountered when a church considers relocating or closing illustrates the significance of the place where the people who share beliefs gather.

Implicit in religion are rewards and punishments. Mainline Protestant congregations do not hear many sermons on heaven and hell these days. Nevertheless, the promise of immortality is clearly there as a reward for the faithful. Whether it is stated explicitly or not, church members anticipate eternal life. The fact that the largest attendance at worship is on Easter when the theme is the resurrection illustrates that the Christian hopes to live forever. There may be other types of explicit rewards, such as the promise that Christians will be better able to cope with life's problems, have more satisfactory marriages, be better adjusted, or simply be happier persons.

The way the local church fulfills these social functions of religion will depend on its theological understanding of the nature and mission of the church. For example, the type of church building that is considered appropriate can vary from a simple Quaker meetinghouse to an elaborate cathedral. Both provide a place for worship and other activities but different theologies dictate that they do it differently. To understand the local church, it is essential to consider how the theological assumptions affect the social functions of religion.

The Local Church as a Social Organization

The local church is a social organization, which is both formal and complex. It has characteristics that can be noted in other social organizations. The first is fixed boundaries; only persons who have met certain criteria are admitted. Churches have requirements for membership, i.e., baptism by immersion, acceptance of a doctrinal statement, or perhaps attendance at a series of training classes or withdrawal from certain activities. The requirements will vary among the denominations and even between churches of the same denomination as a pastor or congregation interprets the requirements with different degrees of strictness. There may also be classifications of membership such as baptized, communicant, active and inactive. It is clear in most churches who is and who is not a member.

A second characteristic of a social organization is the existence of a body of rules or social norms that are accepted as legitimate and supported by the members. Churches often have elaborate sets of rules, *The Book of Discipline of The United Methodist Church* being an example. These define the standards of conduct that are appropriate. A congregation tends to enforce its standards by informal rather than by formal means. Rarely does a person find his or her church membership terminated except for dropping out and then only after a long and complicated process. It is safe to say that virtually anyone who makes an annual financial contribution to a local church can retain membership indefinitely, even if he or she resides across the country. The persons who violate the standards of the congregation will by informal, yet effective means, be made aware of their unacceptability. They may effectively be shut out of the life of the congregation. They will either conform to the group's expectations or simply drop out and in due course be removed from the official roll.

A third characteristic of a complex social organization is that it is a legal system. By this is meant that it has a method for the differentiation of power among the various groups within the organization, a practice that is clearly followed at all levels of Christian denominations. The responsibilities and authority of the clergy and lay officials are spelled out in church law. The United Methodist *Discipline* devotes most of its space to defining the rights and responsibilities of clergy, lay members, local churches, and the multiplicity of other church organizations and agencies.

Fourth, a complex social organization is an association of people engaged in carrying out some form of purposeful activity on a continuous basis. The organization furnishes the people associated with it the means of pursuing their goals. There is often tension in the church because of the wide range of goals that the members have. For example, some persons may be pursuing spiritual goals, finding forgiveness of personal sins and living a holy life; others may see the church as an organization that should be working for specific changes in the larger society. Conflict can arise between those persons who view the church as an instrument to achieve specific goals and those who see participation in the rituals and the fellowship as ends in themselves. Further conflict may occur when the regional or national denominational agencies set goals that may seem unimportant to or in conflict with those of the people in the local churches.

The Community Context

Every local church is located in a community from whose residents it draws members. The community that the average congregation serves can be defined in geographical terms; it is the territory in which the participants live. The extent of a church's service area will be determined by a number of factors including the availability of other congregations of the same or of different denominations, the ease of transportation, and the drawing power of the church's program. Because the church members are expected to participate in worship and other activities on a regular basis, there is a practical limit on how wide an area a local church can serve. Every pastor will tell about a faithful member who travels twenty-five miles each way and never misses a Sunday service. However, a detailed examination of the distribution of participants will usually reveal that the vast majority travel less than ten or fifteen minutes to church.

The local church is to a large degree shaped by the community which it serves, or perhaps more accurately, by that portion of the residents of the community who are its members. Protestant churches tend to serve relatively homogeneous segments of the available population. In a community where the residents are all pretty much alike, as might be found in a new suburb, the church membership would be representative of the entire population. In a more diverse community, such as that served by a downtown church in a large city, the congregation would reflect only a limited segment of the total population.

The individual congregation will have as its potential constituency those persons within the community who may find that type of church meaningful. It does not mean that a particular church can count on some specified portion of the population of a given area. What the congregation does can make the difference as to whether the church has fifty or five hundred people who join. It is not uncommon for a newly established congregation to fail to grow and become financially self-supporting. A denominational executive in referring to such a church lamented, "Aldersgate has everything going for it, a good location and building and a growing community, but it actually lost members last year. It is behind on the mortgage payments and the pastor didn't get a raise in salary." A church's performance depends in part on the community and in part on what the pastor and congregational leaders do to witness and minister in that community.

A present danger among clergy is that they may accept too easily the community as the determining factor as to what a local church cannot do. This becomes a kind of social determinism. An example would be the pastor whose church is located in an area where the population is not growing, or perhaps is declining, and accepts a decreasing membership as normal without considering the proportion of unchurched people in the area. The result can be a self-fulfilling prophecy. The minister assumes that the community determines what the church can or cannot do and acts or fails to act accordingly. The lay members take their cue from the pastor; the congregation soon comes to feel that its options are determined only by external forces. Because the people are convinced that they have limited options, they fail to take initiative. The result can be stagnation with opportunities for ministry irretrievably lost.

It is important that the clergy and the congregation's leaders have a realistic understanding of the community in which its members reside. This will help them determine the best methods of carrying out their mission. It can help prevent fiascoes like the pastor who tried unsuccessfuly to persuade his inner-city congregation to replace their building with a multi-million dollar combination church and office building. But church leaders must also be aware that the community context is only part of the picture. The local church is not like the fast-food outlet whose success is dependent on the volume of traffic that passes by. The effectiveness of the church to a large degree depends on what the people, both lay and clergy, who make up the congregation believe and do in the community where they have been called to witness and serve.

The Local Church's Perception of Its Community

Fundamental to an understanding of the functioning of a local church is the perception of its relationship to the larger community of which it is a part. In the past half century a primary way that the church has understood its relationship to the community was greatly influenced by the sociological studies of Robert E. Park of the University of Chicago. Professor Park studied social characteristics in physical space. Social phenomena (crime, divorce, disease, prostitution, income, education, housing type) were shown on city maps and patterns noted. He was able to present the social characteristics of a geographic community with detail and clarity.

These techniques, which are encompassed by the term *human ecology,* were adopted for local church studies by religious researchers. The assumption was made that a local church had the responsibility to serve all persons within its immediate community. If it did so, the membership would be representative of the community. The congregation would therefore be a microcosm of the larger community, reflecting such characteristics as the age, education, and social class of the residents. Studies compared the congregation with the population of the immediate neighborhood, clearly pointing out which persons in its service area a particular local church was and was not reaching.

The ecological studies of local churches coincided with

the ideal of inclusiveness held by the more liberal denominations. By being able to describe the community with accuracy, it was possible to know the characteristics of the potential members and to design programs that would be appropriate for them. The goal was for each congregation to be representative of its community, including within its membership persons from all racial and socioeconomic groups.

An application of the idea that the congregation should be composed of residents of a geographically defined community is seen in the interdenominational comity agreements that were found in many northern cities during the 1940s and 1950s. Under these plans, a given denomination was assigned a community where it would have the exclusive franchise to organize a new congregation. It was assumed that all present and potential Christians could be served by the church of the denomination to which the community had been assigned. While this was an official policy, denominations managed to organize a sufficient number of new churches so that most residents could find a congregation that suited their tastes and needs.

The ecological studies of local churches were of great importance in demonstrating the characteristics of the communities for which the individual congregations had responsibility. The emphasis on ministering to all the residents of the community certainly helped prevent churches from ignoring segments of the population around them. Every local church must always strive to minister to as broad a range of persons as possible. Yet every church must recognize the validity of other, very different, Christian congregations. It must not suffer feelings of inadequacy, rejection, or guilt when persons select some other church.

CHAPTER 4

The Local Church
as Community

The local church is both a community of people and an institution that exists within the context of a larger community. As a group of people who voluntarily join together, each congregation has a life of its own. It develops a style, which is both similar to and different from other local churches of which it is a part. This chapter will focus on the congregation as a community.

A Voluntary Organization

A fundamental fact of every local church in America is that it is a voluntary organization. People participate and give their time and money because the church is important to them. No one is required to be a member of a church. If any person is unhappy with a particular congregation, he or she may seek another or drop out altogether.

The motivations for attending a particular church are many and complex. The factors that cause an individual to select a particular congregation may include the fact that he or she attended a similar church as a child, the parents were members of the denomination, the doctrine coincides with what the individual believes, or the congregation is a congenial group of people. Many persons do not really think about the reasons why they have selected a particular church; they are simply aware that participation is a significant and meaningful experience.

While the reasons people select a particular church cannot be discerned with any degree of accuracy, one thing is clear. People participate because they are convinced that it is worthwhile for them to do so. It is therefore legitimate to ask what they get in return for their investment of time, energy, and money.

As has already been stated, a fundamental reason for participation in church is the hope of eternal life. A basic theme that runs through most religions is the possibility and nature of life after death. Another reason persons participate in religious activities is to find meaning in life and values by which to live. Human existence is full of uncertainties. Life has a way of abruptly turning corners; the best laid plans can be dashed as tragedy strikes unexpectedly. Religious faith provides a way of understanding life that helps the individual make sense out of existence.

Religion also helps the individual through the transitional periods of life: birth of a child, adulthood, marriage, and death. The church has developed rituals for such occasions, i.e., baptism, confirmation, reception into church membership, marriage, and funerals. The congregation provides a supportive community, which can assist the individual at such times, sharing the joys as well as the sorrows.

Participation in church activities may occur for a variety of reasons other than those listed above. It is, of course, impossible to separate the strictly "religious" rewards from other types of benefits. The newcomer in town may see the church as a good place to meet people; the young adult may be seeking a spouse; the tenor may want a choir in which he can sing. The fact is that the rewards which the individual expects from participating in a church are personal, complex, and difficult to define.

Finally, the voluntary nature of the church means that it has no sanctions. The church cannot force anyone to do anything. It can request, plead, and bring pressure, but the individual is free to act or not act, to participate or to leave. The only thing a church can do is expel someone, something which occurs so rarely that it is newsworthy when it does happen.

The situation is somewhat different in regard to clergy. A denomination, particularly The United Methodist Church, can exercise considerable control over a minister's career. The minister can always leave the denomination or the ministry but he or she may have limited options. It may not be possible to secure employment in another denomination, and the individual may have no training for a position outside the church.

The voluntary nature of the church is both a strength and a weakness. The strength is in the commitment of the people. There is no greater social force than people who are self-motivated. The weakness is that the church can act only to the degree that there is consensus among the members, and it takes time for a group to achieve consensus.

Congregational Homogeneity

The membership of a typical Protestant congregation will be characterized by a high degree of homogeneity. The members will share many common characteristics and while there will be differences, these will tend to be less important than the similarities. Included will be agreement on the theological belief system, type of worship services, church program, and form of church government. Less obvious and acknowledged but of equal importance are a number of social characteristics such as education, income, cultural level, and life-style—factors that tend to be associated with social class.

Each congregation will contain a relatively narrow range of persons when the above criteria are taken into account. While there will be a few people in every congregation who are exceptions to the rule, most of the members will have much in common with the vast majority of the other members. This should not be surprising. The church is a voluntary organization and people tend to join organizations where they perceive the members to be congenial and friendly and to share their own interests. Because of the intimate familylike nature of the church (note the frequency with which a pastor will refer to "the Asbury Church family"), it is important that an individual feel the congregation is made up of persons with whom he or she can be comfortable.

While a detailed examination of virtually any congregation will reveal a high degree of homogeneity, it is a fact that church leaders, particularly the clergy, find this uncomfortable. Christians believe that the gospel is for everyone who will accept it, that Christ died for all. If it is God's will that everyone accept the Christian faith, it would seem to follow that all the believers residing in the same area be in the same church. Most Protestant churches subscribe to the idea that the church, including the local congregation, should be broadly inclusive. Most members see their church as one that is open to any person who wishes to join. They are uncomfortable with the knowledge that their church is not really a group which is broadly diverse.

The idea of homogeneous congregation is not only contrary to our Christian theology but to our democratic ideology as well. American society puts great emphasis on the importance of the individual. Every citizen is perceived to be equal to every other citizen; the one-person-one-vote idea is deep in the nation's tradition. While we know that organizations may be exclusive, we do not like to publicly acknowledge that fact. To admit that a Christian congregation is in fact homogeneous offends both our self-understanding as members of a democratic society and as Christians who believe inclusiveness is a fundamental characteristic of the church.

One group has admitted publicly that congregations are homogeneous. The Church Growth Movement maintains that persons will be attracted to groups made up of people like themselves. Donald McGavran describes this movement in *Church Growth* (Abingdon, 1980) and *Understanding Church Growth* (Eerdmans Publishing Co., 1970). They accept the fact that in a free society people will sort themselves out and affiliate with organizations that meet their needs and provide a meaningful experience. A problem has arisen over the method advocated to produce an increase in local church membership, one which attempts to maximize the homogeneity of the congregation. This method assumes the fact that persons are more likely to affiliate with groups that make them feel comfortable, meaning those in which there are people with whom they have much in common. The charge is made that to consciously attempt to build a congregation of similar people is to promote exclusiveness.

The homogeneity of local congregations explains much about the contemporary church. It is the reason why churches, even those of the same denomination located only a few blocks apart, are not necessarily competing institutions or duplicating each other's ministry. Such congregations may be quite different social groups whose members would not all participate in the same local church. These same congregations may have widely divergent worship practices, programs, and styles of congregational life. Nowhere is this more evident than in The United Methodist Church.

In one city in the Northeast there are two United Methodist churches on the same street less than three blocks apart. One is large, has many of the leading citizens as members and occupies an impressive building. The other has a modest structure and a small membership, which can afford only a part-time pastor. Most of the persons who attend the small church work in the nearby factories. These congregations, which differ greatly from each other, are each homogeneous units.

The homogeneity of local churches explains why congregational mergers so frequently fail. Often the combined congregation after four or five years has about as many members as one of the component parts had when they united. The merging organizations may have been sufficiently different to make their long-term integration impossible. In one midwestern city two congregations of the same denomination merged. The smaller one joined the larger one. However, there was an educational and income difference between the two groups. No member of the smaller church had attended college; a large proportion of the persons in the larger church had done so. While the members of the larger church sincerely welcomed those from the smaller church, the merger failed. Within five years almost all the persons from the smaller church had dropped out or transferred to another congregation. They did not feel at home in the merged congregation with its better educated and more affluent members.

Requisites for Congregational Unity

From its beginning the church has been concerned with unity within the Christian community and within the local congregation. This still is a matter of deep concern to church leaders. There are six requisites for unity within a congregation.[1]

1. *Common Sense of Identity.* The congregation must know who it is and to whom it belongs. It must be able to say clearly, "This is who we are and this is who we are not." Generally, the greater the distinctiveness, or uniqueness a congregation has, the greater the unity among the members.

At one time, Methodists were easily identifiable by their social beliefs (abstinence), their polity (connectionalism), or their worship style ("shouting Methodists" for some; Anglican vestiges for others). Whether they were greatly distinguishable from other Protestant groups, Methodists probably believed that they had a unique witness, heritage, and special perspective on the gospel. The Evangelical United Brethren had not only a distinctive theological position but also an ethnic heritage as well.

As Methodists lost some of their early distinguishing characteristics and became a part of mainline American Protestantism, and as they downplayed their uniqueness in an effort to participate fully in the emerging ecumenical movement, they developed a denominational identity crisis. They had moved from being a sect group with a distinctive identity, to a church with an amorphous, loosely defined identity. As an expression of the catholic spirit within Wesleyan theology and worship, United Methodists have repeatedly told themselves, "After all, we are really very much like everybody else."

Being "like everybody else" nullifies any sense of belonging to an identifiable group.

2. *Common Authority*. There must be some creed, text, person, or constitution to which the congregation ultimately appeals in time of internal crisis, something by which behavior and belief are judged, something or someone which is the final arbiter. This is more than mere bylaws or standard operating procedures; it is the guiding principles, purposes, and goals that name and guide a congregation. This is what makes that gathering a specifically *Christian* gathering, and unites it in hope, purpose, and vision with the church universal.

United Methodists have long had their difficulties with common authority. We recognize and find helpful a variety of historic creeds, but we refuse to consider any of them binding. We have our traditional Articles of Religion, Social Principles, and the Doctrinal Statements, but there are few congregations in which any of these authorities function in any significant way. The Bible is probably the most widely recognized theological authority for United Methodists, but it is an authority that functions in a flexible, *ad hoc* manner. It is not accepted as the rigid and complete authority on all matters.

A congregation that suffers from a lack of common authority will find its life affected in several ways. Without a recognized authority to which everyone can refer and defer, it is difficult to deal constructively with differences of opinion. It is impossible to resolve an argument if we cannot appeal to some commonly recognized source or validation for differing points of view. Debate is carefully avoided out of fear that the debate will be divisive rather than productive. The congregation attempts to keep everything polite, genteel, and cheerful lest, during a difference of opinion, the group should fall apart, because there is no commonly agreed upon authority to which differing points of view can appeal.

For a congregation, authority is not an optional matter. Congregations that lose the Bible or any other historic, basic, creedal-type statement of faith are forced to seek their common authority elsewhere. Authority may come to reside in the congregation's pastor, or in some lay leader of the congregation. Secular, generalized, culturally defined standards may become normative for the congregation: "It really doesn't matter what any of us believes as long as we are sincere." Methodists believe in "think and let think!" Unity thus becomes a matter of congeniality rather than a matter of shared faith. When a congregation's authority is little more than an *ad hoc*, locally sanctioned, idiosyncratic, vague consensus among its members of "what seems right to us," the group cannot know that its work and witness are specifically Christian.

3. *Common Memory.* The congregation must have a shared story, a common history through which it understands itself and its mission. Every unified group, which exists beyond one generation, places great emphasis on its history. The history will begin orally with charter members recounting for new or younger members "the way things used to be." Early struggles, founding fathers and mothers, original buildings and furnishings will all be treated with reverence. There will be denominational heroes as well as congregational heroes for succeeding generations to emulate. The common history gives a congregation its roots, its identity, its authority.

There are certain factors that tend to disrupt or at least devalue a congregation's common memory. We live in a uniquely ahistorical culture, which tends to value youth and newness over age and oldness. We are a young, adolescent nation where great concern for the past is often judged to be mere antiquarianism or backward-looking conservatism.

Within the congregation, a number of factors contribute to a further devaluation of the common memory. We are a mobile society. In many congregations, there is a constant influx of new members accompanied by the departure of old members. Few old-timers are left to tell the congregation's story and few want to hear that story. Newcomers are often threatened by old-timers' attempts to recount congregational history, feeling that, since they have not intimately shared in the history, the history excludes them from full congregational participation. In addition, pastors within United Methodist congregations are sometimes apathetic or hostile to a congregation's history. United Methodist pastors belong to the Annual Conference, not to the congregations which they serve. A pastor's tenure at a given congregation may be relatively short. United Methodist ministers are in for difficulty if they start looking upon the individual congregation as their source of identity and primary locus of ministry. In a few years, the pastors will move to other congregations. Therefore, the history of a congregation is usually viewed by pastors as the property of that congregation.

Some pastors appear to be threatened by a congregation's common story, probably for the same reason that other newcomers may be threatened. The story can be a way of excluding new members, including the new minister. This may be why many pastors deliberately devalue or ignore congregational traditions, common memories, yearly celebrations, and cherished patriarchs. Such activities possess a power and a pervasive influence that the pastor does not control.

Common memories become dysfunctional in a congregation's life when they are ignored or transgressed by new members or new pastors. The old-timers react with hostility, rigidity, and entrenchment. Their reaction may arise because the old-timers instinctively sense that, if they lose their common story, they will lose something that is part of the basic fabric of the congregation's existence. Common memories should be used rather than abused. Memories can be powerful motivators for behavior. Memory of past events can become a rallying point for creative and adaptive behavior in the present.

New members or new pastors in a congregation should expect a time of formal or informal instruction by the old-timers in a congregation's common memories. This is not only an attempt on the part of the old-timers to assert their authority as old-timers but also an attempt to integrate new members into the present life of the congregation. In fact, congregations, especially larger and more transient congregations, would be wise to intentionally instruct, through new members' classes, a congregational handbook, congregational sponsors of new members, newcomers in the congregation's common memories.

4. *Common Vision.* The congregation must share common goals and guides for which it lives and by which it lives. As a common memory identifies where the congregation has been, so a common vision identifies where the congregation should be or hopes to be in the future.

Currently, there has been much stress upon goal-setting and planning in The United Methodist Church. This process can foster congregational consensus and a sense of ownership for activities and programs. Goals can help a congregation be specific and realistic in its expectations for the future. Evaluation of the goals at the end of a designated period can also give a congregation a much needed sense of accomplishment. However, defining congregational direction solely in terms of specific, definable, achievable, and measurable goals can limit a local church's vision to the operational, the pragmatic, and the reasonable. The Christian vision, in its congregational or worldwide expressions, is inherently unrealistic by many of the world's standards. Christian expectations are eschatological, beyond the confines of the present time and our present programs for human betterment. An ordained Christian leader is inherently more than a mere congregational manager or setter of congregational goals. The pastor is also a visionary, a dreamer of dreams, and an interpreter of dreams.

Also, without sufficient common memory and common authority, a congregation's goals will be questionable. How will the congregation judge its achievable, understandable, measurable goals and visions and determine if they are *Christian?* When a congregation lacks a common locus of identity, authority, and memory that is beyond itself and tied to the historic witness of the church, its goals and visions easily become a 10 percent increase in the budget, a net gain of fifteen new members, a new air conditioning system, rather than an increase among men of the love of God and neighbor, or the making of disciples for Jesus Christ.

A common vision is essential to the vitality and unity of a congregation. Unfortunately, as a congregation or a denomination matures, its vision tends to blur. The vision that originally motivated the founders becomes trimmed down and adjusted to the realities of the contemporary world. Momentum is lost and the congregation or the denomination cares less about using itself for the future and more about preserving its life in the present. Perhaps The United Methodist Church and its congregations are experiencing this inevitable maturing and blurring of vision today. But while United Methodists struggle with their vision, there is little evidence that humanity in general is less concerned with vision. The resurgence of apocalypticism, the rising cult of the futurist, the appearances of strange messianic groups all testify to the continuing need of people to envision a future, to set meaningful goals, and to venture forth confidently into that future.

5. *Common Shared Life Together.* A congregation must share the intimacy, relatedness, and mutual feeling that is the visible sign to the world of the presence of the kingdom of God in our midst. While the mere presence of friendliness is not a guarantee that the congregation is specifically *Christian,* it is interesting that many people join and remain in churches because of a congregation's alleged friendliness. We are a nation that is caught between its strong individualism and a deep yearning for community. There can be no doubt that many people seek a church and join a church because they are lonely and yearn to be a part of a group that cares, regardless of that group's theological commitments or lack of them.

Usually, there is a fair amount of infighting and bickering in a congregation, which shows a firm sense of common shared life together. But this can be a positive sign. A congregation that has little in common, which is unsure of its cohesiveness and unity, cannot afford to tolerate conflict for fear that the congregation will fall apart. A closely unified congregation not only loves like a family but also fights like a family. Intimacy, in families or in congregations, can lead to conflict. Sometimes members are so continually close that they know all too well one another's strengths and weaknesses. But the conflict can be productive. At least people care enough to fight about things!

6. *Common Shared Life in the World.* A Christian congregation is called to be more than an isolated enclave of like-minded friends. A church is also called to be a

visible witness to the ever-coming kingdom of God in the world.

When congregational togetherness becomes narcissistic self-infatuation, something is wrong. The church exists between the tension of being not of the world and yet also called to win and transform the world. Unfortunately, in recent years, many have come to believe that a concern for congregational unity and cohesiveness is antithetical to concern with serving the world. Congregations who take congregational unity with great seriousness are accused of being turned in on themselves, indifferent to the needs and hurts of the world around them.

A congregation must love itself before it is capable of loving others. A congregation will not love its neighbors in a vibrant, committed way until it has first learned to love its own witness, its own tradition, its own message, its own life together. A congregation must first be confident and optimistic about itself before it will be motivated to share itself with the world. In fact, before it experiences the gospel within its own congregational life, a congregation more than likely has no gospel to share with anyone else.

Meaningful congregational involvement in ministry to the world, especially when that involvement arises out of a church's identity and vocation, can be a source of congregational unity. Even when that involvement brings conflict, a congregation's response to the conflict can promote a more unified body. The conflict can provide an occasion for working through a congregation's identity and faith. It can result in commitment, risk, and involvement, which become part of the congregation's memory, a warmly remembered time when the congregation experienced itself, not only as a unified group, but also as a visible witness to the kingdom of God in the world.

PART II

The Functioning
of the
Local United Methodist Church

CHAPTER 5

Entering and Leaving

Christianity by its very nature has been evangelistic. The commandment to "Go into all the world . . ." is a central tenet of the tradition. Christians, convinced that they had found salvation, wanted others to have it too. Acceptance of the Christian faith has led to membership in some group, usually a local church where the convert was instructed and nurtured.

Any social institution, including the church, must continually secure new members. Churches have approached this differently. Some have been willing to depend for members on persons born into church families and brought up in the faith. Others aggressively seek converts from among persons who are unchurched or who are members of churches of other denominations.

United Methodism is the product of a revival. Whatever else John Wesley may have been, he was first an evangelist whose preaching brought his hearers under the conviction of sin and moved them to repentance. He was also an organizer who provided a structure for the nurture, support, and discipline of the convert. The persons who were converted to Christianity under Methodist preachers were not left to their own resources but taken under the care and supervision of a society.

Today evangelism is much in the thinking of United Methodists as they analyze the causes of the membership decrease in the period since the 1968 Methodist–Evangelical United Brethren merger and consider what might be done to reverse this trend.

The admission of new members takes place in the thousands of local churches as persons stand before the congregation to affirm their faith and pledge that they shall be loyal to The United Methodist Church and support it by their prayers, presence, gifts, and service. However, membership is not perceived to be the result of one's conversion to Christianity; an acceptance of the faith is assumed. In many United Methodist congregations the impression is given that formal membership is the goal, because little or no attention is paid to the understanding of or commitment to the Christian faith. The future of the denomination will be determined not only by the effectiveness with which the pastor and people in the thousands of congregations recruit church members but also in the way these new members understand and act out their faith.

This chapter will consider how people enter and leave the congregation, including the role of the minister and the laity in bringing new people into the congregation, the different levels of membership that the individual can attain, and the reason and way membership is terminated.

Admission into the Congregation

A local church is both one of the easiest and one of the most difficult organizations to join. It is easy in that virtually any person, who has been or is willing to be baptized, indicates a belief in the basic doctrines, and promises to be loyal and to support the church, will be received. An individual who is a member of another congregation of the same or a different denomination will be received by letter of transfer with virtually no questions asked.

The United Methodist congregation that insists on a long period of training during which the beliefs of the church are explained to the prospective member is indeed rare. Rarer still is the pastor or congregation who examines the prospective member on his or her faith. Some local churches do have classes for new members, but these tend to be orientation sessions to introduce the newcomers to the program of that particular congregation. These classes are not a screening process, which results in applicants either changing their minds or being deried membership. In United Methodism the pastor decides who shall be admitted into membership, and most pastors are more anxious to secure members than to examine prospects on the depth of their commitment. Rare indeed is the person who cannot find an accommodating minister when he or she wants to join a church.

While joining a church or getting one's name on the official roll is easy, becoming an integral part of the congregation can be difficult and take a long time. Congregations, particularly smaller congregations, which are the majority of Protestant churches, are like an extended family. Friendships are the product of long periods of association. The members will have shared many experiences, such as the struggle to erect the education wing or the conflict over whether to buy a new parsonage. They may have worked together as they taught each other's children in the Sunday school, shared in each other's joys at the baptism or wedding of a child, and provided comfort and support when a member died. People cannot join a family; they must be adopted. While it is easy to simply join the church, it can be much more difficult to be adopted by the group, to become a part of an intimate familylike fellowship.

The entrance of a newcomer can be disruptive to a social group. It not only adds someone who does not share the experiences of the members but also someone who may challenge the patterns of relationships and leadership. The group may effectively shut out persons who it feels will be disruptive or who do not share the values and ideals of the members.

Every church has a self-image of being open, friendly, and anxious to welcome visitors and receive newcomers. Visitors are given red ribbons so they can be identified and welcomed. But churches are often not as open as the members think they are. A seminary student working in a church for the summer commented:

> Bethel Church thinks it's open and friendly. They make a big fuss over any out-of-town visitors who attend. We had a vacationing preacher from Pennsylvania, and they gave him and his family a warm reception. They did the same when my parents visited me. However, I've observed that when local people, persons who might actually join, visit, the response is likely to be less cordial. Actually they seem to freeze some of the local folks out.

Recruiters or Gatekeepers

The pastor is often the chief recruiter of new members. The importance that the minister attaches to winning members and his or her ability to persuade persons to join the church may mean the difference between a growing and declining membership. The pastor tends to set the example for the laity. When the minister gives leadership in winning persons to Christ and to church membership, laypersons will be more likely to witness to their faith and seek to persuade persons to join the church. The result can be an enthusiastic and growing congregation.

There are several reasons why the clergy are crucial in winning members. The minister is often the first representative of the church that a newcomer encounters. If the first contact is by attending a worship service, the visitor hears the minister preach. Attendance at church may be followed by a pastoral call, which gives the newcomer another opportunity to assess the minister. The personality and skill of the pastor may determine whether the individual joins that church or looks further.

While it would be rare for a congregation without the participation and encouragement of the clergy to actively seek members, the cooperation of the laity is essential. While the clergy may persuade persons to join the church, they cannot make a new member an integral part of the fellowship. It is the laypersons who determine whether the new member is received into the church and becomes a part of its vital life or remains on the fringe. The members of a congregation decide who shall be admitted into the inner circle. They may not discuss the matter, take a formal vote, or even be aware of the process, but the end result is the same. The fact is that persons select and are accepted by a congregation where the members can share some of the most significant events in each other's lives. The minister may get persons onto the rolls but only the layperson can really admit them into the fellowship.

The most successful outreach is that accomplished by the laity. When the lay members recruit members, the newcomers are already well on their way to becoming an integral part of the congregation. A pastor of a downtown church in a small city discovered that his church had relatively few married young adults. Determined to change this situation, he recruited several couples and helped them initiate activities of interest to that age group. After about a year he reported, "The young adults have become an active group and a significant part of our congregation. Like seems to attract like; they are now finding other young adults and bringing them into the church."

A Method for Decision-Making

A major problem in securing acceptance of the Christian faith and a commitment to the church is the lack of a method for decision-making. The revival or series of evangelistic services was for a long period in United Methodism the way individuals were confronted with the claims of the gospel and given an opportunity to make a decision to accept or not accept Christ. The series of services with the preacher presenting the reality of sin and calling for repentance, the pressure of the church members as they prayed for and labored with the lost to get them to the altar, made the revival a time when decisions were made. When the repentant sinner responded to the altar call and came forward to pray and receive forgiveness, it was a public event. The whole community was aware of what had occurred; everyone could affirm the decision and support the new convert. Furthermore, it was difficult for the individual to backslide after having made a public decision to become a Christian.

The revival meeting has all but disappeared from the mainline churches, although it is still found in some denominations. When a United Methodist church has what may still be called a revival, it is usually a series of services conducted by a neighboring pastor and has neither the fervor nor pressure for decisions typical of the old-style evangelism. The church of course cannot or should not attempt to return to the old methods. Nevertheless, the contemporary church has not yet found a socially acceptable substitute for the mourners' bench. There is currently no method for helping persons make a decision to accept the Christian faith that involves the congregation. The individual may respond to a particular sermon but this is a private response. The pastor in private conversation may press for a commitment. Decisions may occur in a church school class or a prayer group; other members of the congregation may not share or even be aware of this event.

Levels of Membership

There are various levels of church membership that an individual may attain. These are not formal stages but an informal process by which the newcomer becomes an integral part of a congregation. This can be visualized as several levels of involvement ranging from very little to a high level of participation in the life of the congregation.

These different degrees of membership tend to be more evident in the larger churches than in the smaller. It is impossible for the individual to hide in a small congregation. If the membership is less than a hundred, it is obvious to everyone who is and is not participating. This is one reason why small churches will have a larger proportion of the members attending than will large congregations.

Carl S. Dudley has compared the small church to a single-cell organism with every member being an integral part of the organization. In contrast the large church will consist of many suborganizations; the average person will participate in several but no one will be a member of all of them. The person who joins a large congregation can decide how deeply to become involved while the new member of the small church may not have this option. He or she must either be a part of the single-cell organization or remain on the outside.

The level of membership that an individual attains depends on two factors: the person's desire to become an integral part of the congregation and the degree of openness of the members to bringing new people into their group. The person who wants to be an integral part of the congregation must take the initiative in participating in activities. The newcomer can participate more easily in some church activities than in others. Volunteers for the annual bazaar or the spring clean-up days are always welcome. It is usually easier to become a church school teacher than it is to be elected to the Finance Committee or to the Board of Trustees.

Most church people are not aware of how difficult it is for the newcomer to become a vital part of the congregation. Because the members all know one another, they tend to presume that anyone can easily become a part of the fellowship. It is assumed that the congregation is open to all, but little may be done to communicate this fact. For example, there are thousands of churches whose outdoor signboards do not even give the times of the services; anyone wishing to attend would have to take the initiative to find this information.

Some churches have a kind of informal apprenticeship before persons will be elected to an office, particularly the more prestigious positions such as membership on the governing board. At one congregational meeting a lady began her remarks by saying, "I'm still a newcomer in this church; I've only been a member for eleven years." A result of such a practice is to fail to use the talents of a significant portion of the members and miss the infusion of new ideas so vital to the life of a congregation. It is important for both pastors and laity to realize how closed a group or local church can become, even inadvertently. They can then determine whether they are content with the situation or wish to alter it.

Leaving the Church

Persons drop out of church for personal and complex reasons. This makes it impossible to generalize on the subject. It appears that most persons do not stop participating because of internal conflict. The member who gets involved in a congregational conflict is one who tends to have strong feeling about the church; the last thing he or she wants to do is leave.

There are a number of reasons why persons drop out or drift away from church while still residing in the same community. These may include a change in the individual's family. A couple may be divorced or widowed; the children may have grown up and left home. The routine of family life is changed and this can result in change in other relationships, including church participation.

Persons who have been intensely involved in church activities may become fatigued or experience a kind of burnout. After years of serving on committees and teaching a church school class, some persons appear to become tired or bored and simply drop out. They develop an attitude of letting someone else assume the responsibilities.

Another reason why members drop out of a local church is that the church itself may change so that it no longer meets their needs. The program emphases may change with the assignment of a new pastor. These will not occur immediately but a minister can make significant changes in three or four years. Hence members who found certain activities meaningful may drop out when the program is changed. The personality of the minister is an important factor. Some persons may so dislike a particular minister that they cease attending church; some do not return even when the pastor leaves.

An example of the impact of the clergy can be noted in a midwestern congregation. A pastor with a great commitment to social action and an abrasive personality was assigned to a growing congregation. He led the church into some highly controversial programs. While he enlisted the support of some persons with similar interests, he lost others who were not in sympathy with his emphasis. In due course the minister was replaced by a rather plodding, uninspiring traditional pastor. This displeased the social activists who tended to drift away. By the time the second man had served four years, the congregation had declined to the point of crisis.

Not attending worship or participating in other church activities does not terminate one's membership. Local churches are quick to add persons to the membership rolls, but they are most reluctant to remove the names of persons who have moved away or have become inactive. The ease with which persons are admitted is in sharp contrast with the resistance to dismissing inactive members.

Persons can, of course, request that their membership be transferred to another church; such a request will be immediately honored. A member may withdraw or resign from the congregation. This simply terminates the relationship, leaving the individual free to affiliate or not to affiliate with some other church at some time in the future. However, few persons withdraw from a local church; they simply stop participating. It is what to do about the inactive members that seems to cause so much anguish among United Methodist leaders.

Every congregation has some persons on the roll who no longer participate. These include children of church families who are in college and persons who have moved away but still want to maintain their affiliation with their home church. These persons should be retained; many will eventually affiliate with a congregation somewhere.

There will also be a number of nonresident members with whom the church has lost contact; it may not have a current address for some of these. Others will reside in the community but for some reason have dropped out of the congregation. It is these persons that the denomination seems most reluctant to remove from the rolls. The current procedure is complex and requires three years before membership can be terminated.

The high level of resistance to removing someone from the membership is caused by several factors. The first is a genuine concern for the persons who have dropped out of the church and a desire that they maintain a meaningful faith and membership in a congregation. The second is the sense of failure and guilt that leaders feel when the church is in fact rejected by the person who slips away. They feel they have somehow failed, that if they had done a better job of presenting the gospel and nurturing the persons, the members would not have dropped out. While this may or may not be the case, the way church leaders feel about the dropouts account in part for the unwillingness to remove their names from the roll. A final factor is the reluctance by some judicatory leaders to have the membership in their area decrease; local churches are in fact discouraged from dropping inactive persons.

The unfortunate result of this practice is that it places a false emphasis on statistics. It encourages pastors to be a bit dishonest by allowing the church rolls to be inflated with the names of persons who are no longer active or reside in the community. It tends to say to the clergy and the laity that membership size is the most important criterion of success. Finally, it gives a false sense of well-being and, like the patient who refuses to admit an illness, may prevent necessary corrective action.

The present practice of easy admission into church membership coupled with a complex procedure for removing someone from the church roll is one of the indications that United Methodism has moved all the way from sect to church. The discipline required to be a member of a Methodist society has long since given way to membership in a church where the standards for admission are not uniformly interpreted or enforced and where the institution is most reluctant to let members be removed, even if they do not participate and cannot be located.

This has resulted both from the growth of Methodism and from the changing understanding of what it means to be a church member. It is impossible to maintain the disciplined religious life in a large institution that was possible in small societies. Many local churches must struggle to have the members get acquainted with one another; the mutual concern for each other's spiritual development and righteous living has with rare exceptions been abandoned. As Methodism moved from a reform movement within a denomination to a broadly inclusive church, its theology of church membership has become easier to acquire and harder to lose. There is the belief that joining a church will lead to conversion and growth in the Christian life, an assumption that does not necessarily follow.

CHAPTER 6

Clergy and Laity

Two United Methodist laypersons were discussing their pastor. One commented, "I have really appreciated Bill; he is a fine preacher and he has been good for our church. But he is now in his fifth year and there is a strong possibility that he will move in June. I wish the bishop would leave him here at least another year."

A lay member who was extremely dissatisfied with her pastor sought out the chairman of the Pastor-Parish Relations Committee to explain why that group should request a change of ministers. The response of the chairman was, "George is at the end of his third year with us so there is a good chance that he will move in another year. Besides, he is better than the last minister we had."

The two conversations are illustrations of the single most important factor in determining the relationship between United Methodist ministers and the lay members of their local churches. The United Methodist minister is a member of an Annual Conference and is appointed to a local church within that Annual Conference by a bishop. While the congregation through the Pastor-Parish Relations Committee is consulted, neither the committee nor the congregation has final authority in determining which minister shall be assigned to the church. The authority of the Annual Conference over the careers of the clergy forms the basis for clergy-lay relationships within the local church.

The Minister's Home Base

The United Methodist pastor is a member of an Annual Conference that encompasses a geographic area such as all of Iowa or half of Mississippi. Although transfers between Annual Conferences are possible, the vast majority of clergy spend all of their careers serving churches within the same conference. It is the clergy members of the Annual Conference who determine who shall be admitted into the ministry. The bishop then assigns ministers to local churches with the denomination guaranteeing them an appointment as long as they remain members of the Annual Conference in good standing.

The minister's official tie with the church is through membership in the Annual Conference, not in the local congregation. The clergy's primary loyalty tends to be to the Annual Conference, not to the congregation. It is after all the Annual Conference in which the minister has his or her career. Promotions generally come to the United Methodist pastor by appointments to larger churches. The decisions concerning who will receive the promotions are not made by laypersons on a call committee but by denominational officials. While the pastor's past performance will be a major factor in making assignments, the decisions are made by persons who are themselves clergy. For the clergy the Annual Conference has the characteristics of a closed shop union and it receives their allegiance.

The United Methodist minister's membership in an Annual Conference provides the individual with a degree of security not found in many other denominations. It guarantees freedom of the pulpit by protecting the pastor from arbitrary dismissal because of an unpopular stand on a controversial issue. The minister has the assurance that if the congregation does insist on a move, the Annual Conference will provide an appointment at another church. While it protects the prophet, membership in the Annual Conference can also protect the incompetent pastor. One of the weaknesses in the system is the virtual impossibility of terminating an ineffective minister who is not guilty of misconduct. Clergy who are unproductive or even incompetent, or as one bishop used to say, "persons who overheard someone else's call to preach," will be carried by the United Methodist system. Such persons may move frequently among the lower-paying churches but year after year they will continue to receive an appointment.

The privileges and advantages that the ministers receive are not without their cost. These include the willingness to place the decisions as to where they will serve in the hands of the denominational officials. The United Methodist pastor cannot openly seek a specific church or negotiate the terms of employment with a congregation. Being a part of an itinerant system requires a willingness to move, often on short notice, to the assigned church wherever it is located. Finally, the United Methodist system tends to limit rapid upward mobility. The younger pastor, however talented, rarely receives an appointment to a large prestigious church, but with each move is assigned to a slightly larger congregation.

Because the clergy's home is the Annual Conference, they can usually be counted on to support the actions and programs of the denomination, even if these are in conflict with the wishes of the members of the local church. Failure to support the Annual Conference program and fund-raising goals is viewed by most pastors as being hazardous to their careers, a perception that is not incorrect. An accepted fact among United Methodist clergy is that the individual who wishes to advance will be sure the congregation pays the full amount of money requested by the denomination for its administrative overhead and benevolent programs.

United Methodist clergy tend to move frequently; four to six years is considered an appropriate term although many terms are less than four years. This reinforces the pastors' feeling that the Annual Conference is their home base rather than the local church. The ministers and the laypersons know there will be a different pastor in a relatively short time. The clergy may avoid dealing with a difficult situation and simply let it wait for the next person appointed to the church. Laypersons tend to be unwilling to deal with a problem pastor or one who is incompetent, preferring to avoid conflict by putting up with him or her for a year or two until a different person is assigned.

Democratic But Clergy Dominated

Most United Methodists would insist that their church is democratic and in the main they would be correct. The voting members of the Annual Conferences are one-half clergy and one-half laity. However, the Charge Conference that is the governing body of the local church is a small group of congregational officers who represent the total membership. While there is provision for a congregational meeting, it occurs only infrequently. Most church people, however, would insist that there is adequate opportunity for all members to make their views heard and to influence the course of their congregation.

The clergy control the Annual Conference and tend to exercise a dominant influence in the local church. The Annual Conference is, after all, the ministers' professional organization; they are likely to be in attendance and familiar with the issues under consideration. In the local church the matter is more complex. The laypersons may exercise considerable control but there are several factors that enable the clergy to be dominant.

The first, which is not limited to United Methodism, is the tendency of many laypersons not to question or at least be reluctant to question the authority of an ordained minister. There is a kind of "halo effect" around the minister so that to challenge the pastor, even on a mundane matter of church business, may seem a bit like challenging God. A result is that the clergy are given considerable authority within the congregation. The second factor that increases the control of the clergy is the structure of the local church. The annual business meeting or Charge Conference, which sets the budget, elects the officers, and determines congregational policies and programs, is a small body consisting of the local church officials. Furthermore, the persons presented to the Charge Conference for election to the various congregational offices are chosen by a Nominating Committee of which the pastor is chairperson. The minister therefore has a major voice in the selection of the members who will hold office. While it is possible to nominate persons from the floor and overrule the Nominating Committee, rarely does this occur.

The main advantage of this aspect of the United Methodist system is its efficiency. It places the decision-making authority in a group of church officials whose selection is made by a committee chaired by the pastor. A quorum is those persons present after due notice of the Charge Conference has been given. It is assumed that this group of local church officials will reflect the sentiments of the majority. While decisions can be made efficiently, there is the danger that control will be exercised by an oligarchy dominated by the pastor with a large proportion of the members not participating and not having a sense of ownership for the program of their church.

Another way by which The United Methodist Church tends to continue clergy dominance is that when a layperson becomes serious about the Christian faith, he or she is often encouraged to assume some of the functions of the ordained clergy. The service that laypersons perform as dedicated workers in the congregation, such as teaching a church school class or visiting the nonchurched in the community, however, is not perceived to be as significant as what the ordained clergy do. The active layperson may be encouraged to become a lay speaker and supply the pulpit in small churches either on an occasional or regular basis. The individual may be encouraged to become an unordained local pastor and serve as the minister of a small congregation on either a part-time or a full-time basis. While many such persons provide effective service to the churches, the system tends to convey to laypersons that the real Christian is the individual who has entered some form of the professional or quasi-professional ministry. Service provided by lay members is perceived to be of a lesser order than that of the clergy. It has the effect of helping assure the clergy's position of dominance in the church.

Dependence on the Clergy

The United Methodist system, particularly the appointment of ministers by a bishop, tends to make the local church more dependent on the clergy than is the case in some other denominations. When a pastor dies or leaves the ministry, the congregation goes into a holding pattern. Everything other than the routine services await the appointment of a replacement. With its efficient system of clergy placement, the Annual Conference will see that a new minister is on the scene almost immediately. The assignment of a permanent replacement may set off a chain reaction; several pastors may move up to slightly larger churches. This is usually the case if a large church becomes vacant. An interim minister may be assigned when a small congregation loses its pastor. This may be a retired minister who can serve until the next session of the Annual Conference, the time when persons are received into the ministry and appointments made. The United Methodist system is in contrast to those denominations in which churches may take from six to fifteen months to call a minister. In such churches the laypersons are deeply involved. The process often includes a congregational self-study to help the people determine the kind of pastor needed. In United Methodism the bishop and the district superintendents tend to rely on their knowledge of the local church in order to decide the type of pastor to be assigned. There is not the in-depth study that enables a congregation to assess its needs and determine its goals.

The question can be raised as to whether the average United Methodist local church is more dependent on its minister than is one with a congregational polity. The critical factor is the laypersons' perception of their role in the governing of the congregation. United Methodism stresses the primacy of the connection and not the local congregation. United Methodists are made aware that they are members of the entire connection and not just their local church. This contributes to a situation where the church members look for and accept direction from the denomination to a degree that can stifle initiative at the local level. It results in the laity's being overly dependent on the clergy and on the denomination. It may prevent the members from having a sense of ownership for their church and its program.

Appointments and Income

The United Methodist system of having a panel of experts (the bishop and district superintendents) assign the pastors should in theory make it possible to match the skills of the minister with the needs of the congregation. With an appointive system the type of pastor a congregation needs at a given time can be assigned. The bishop can theoretically select any minister from among the several hundred members of the Annual Conference.

In actual fact, the choices of the bishop are much more limited. First, he can select from among only those clergy who are available to move, which would exclude those who had recently relocated. More important is the practice of moving ministers to a church that pays a salary somewhat higher than his or her present church. Unless the individual has been guilty of misconduct resulting in a demotion, the next appointment will not pay a lower salary than the amount currently being received. Futhermore, there is great resistance against providing too large an increase for the incoming pastor. In making appointments some cabinets (the bishop and the district superintendents) work from a list arraying the pastors by their salaries from the highest to the lowest. Also included may be church membership and the way the congregation paid its apportionments for denominational administration and benevolences in the preceding year.

Thus, when a church becomes vacant, the persons in the salary bracket just below what that church is paying are the ones considered. In most cases someone from this group will be selected. This will set off a kind of chain reaction, which involves the moving of several pastors with each one moving up one step in the salary scale. Thus the local congregation unknowingly finds itself locked into a system where the pastors eligible for appointment to that church are determined by the salary they are willing to pay. But the congregation cannot secure the pastor it desires simply by raising the salary. Offering a higher salary will eliminate a group of clergy who are perceived as not eligible for such a large increase in salary.

The present system has perpetuated one of the most destructive myths in United Methodism. This is the idea that the higher salary a local church provides the better pastor it is certain to secure. While many able persons do find their way to the larger churches with the high salaries, there are other persons who simply get aboard the escalator and are carried upward. Pastors sometimes encourage congregations to increase their salaries by telling them that this is the best way to guarantee that the church will receive a person of ability at the time of the next move. For a minister to claim that an increase in salary will assure a competent successor at the next change is self-seeking.

Laypersons are puzzled when they provide a high salary and their next minister does not live up to their expectations of excellence. One such person questioned "We pay one of the better salaries in the district and look who the bishop sent. Aren't there any better men in this conference?" What this individual did not realize was that their pastor, a loyal member of the Annual Conference, had arrived in the salary bracket of that church. He needed to move and the church needed a pastor. Commenting about the same pastor, the district super- intendent asked, "What am I going to do with a man who has flopped to the top?"

Accountability

The United Methodist connectional system has been an efficient and effective way of deploying clergy and mobilizing a body of Christian people to carry out the mission of the church. The system requires that the clergy be able to itinerate (move) and be willing to accept the assignment given by the bishop. It also requires that the clergy be responsible to one another for their conduct; the group then insures that each member maintains appropriate moral standards.

As the total number of clergy and the size of the Annual Conferences have increased, the Annual Confer- ences have changed from brotherhoods where the clergy all knew one another to become professional associations. The kind of covenant that the ministers previously made to one another no longer exists. One result is that there is no longer the kind of mutual accountability for conduct and performance that existed when the organizations were smaller. It is almost impossible to monitor colleagues' performance and to discipline them if they fail to meet the required standards when the total group is large and many members are not well acquainted with one another. With a system that is dominated by the ordained ministers and highly protective of its members, there is the danger that the care and support of the clergy will become the primary mission of the church. The increasing expectations of the clergy for benefits and privileges indicate that the trend is moving in that direction. This situation is serious but probably not as bad as one district superintendent observed, "The clergy union is wrecking The United Methodist Church."

It is crucial that laypersons take more responsibility for the management and programs of the local church and for holding the clergy accountable. There are, of course, many United Methodist ministers who encourage the laypersons to take such initiative. Only strong and secure persons are willing to do so. They must go against the prevailing current, which tends to put the initiative in the various denominational organizations, and a system that tends to be dominated by the clergy. Furthermore, they must often convince laypersons to assume the responsibilities of leadership that demand time, energy, and a willingness to deal with difficult and conflict situations. Nevertheless, the church cannot function effectively if it is dominated by the clergy with the laypersons passively depending on the ministers to provide the direction. The church needs the leadership as well as the support of its laity.

The latter part of the twentieth century will be remembered as a time when individuals felt they should be making more of the decisions that affect their lives. This trend can be noted among the United Methodist clergy who are pressing for a greater voice in the choice of their appointment. It is also beginning to be present among the laypeople. The recently added requirement that both the minister and the local church be consulted regarding a proposed appointment is an example of this trend. Increased tension between the laypersons and the clergy will certainly result if the members of both groups continue to insist on a greater voice in the appointment of the pastor of a local church.

Loyalty to institutions can no longer be taken for granted, and this includes loyalty to both the local church and to the denomination. An example is the amount of church shopping families do when they move into a new community. While they probably start with the congregations of the denomination of which they are members, most do not hesitate to choose a church of another mainline denomination in which the clergy are dominant. This increasing desire of people to want to share in the decision-making and the decreasing institutional loyalty will mean that such churches cannot count on a faithful and docile clientele. A more nearly equal partnership between laity and clergy must be forged, a process that will not be without tension and conflict.

There are certain risks in working toward a church in which the clergy are less dominant. More laypersons may actually begin to exercise power. They may make mistakes; they may subscribe to a theology that is perceived to be too conservative or certainly different from what is being taught in the schools of theology. They may challenge and change the accepted ways of doing things; they may even become enthusiastic and excited about their religion.

Christianity is, after all, too important to be left solely to the clergy. The significant participation of large numbers of laypersons in the operation of the local church and the denomination may be just what is needed to challenge the clergy and to shake the denomination out of its doldrums.

CHAPTER 7

The Local Church and
the Denomination

"The primary mark of United Methodism as a church is that it is a connection. . . . it is a unity of which the respective Jurisdictional, Central, and Annual conferences and the various local churches are only local manifestations."[1]

The term *connectionalism,* which United Methodists use to describe their church, is a concept that is difficult to define but one that United Methodists believe to be a unique characteristic of their denomination. Local churches are not perceived as autonomous units, which choose to relate to one another (which is the pattern of congregational bodies). Nor do they see their denomination as being subject to a hierarchy with authority in a person as in the Roman Catholic Church. Connectionalism refers to a kind of voluntary unity that has certain tangible manifestations in the manner by which Methodist people and congregations relate to each other, and the way the individual parts assume a degree of mutual responsibility and accountability to the larger group.

The Background

The word *connection* used to describe Methodism goes back to the days of the denomination's origins. Originally the Methodist movement was simply the sum of those local groups or classes whose members and lay preachers had chosen to become associated with John Wesley. He was in a very real sense the connection between them. While Wesley regularly conferred with his associates, there was no question that he was the person in charge. He made the final decisions. The person who joined the Methodist movement voluntarily accepted Wesley's authority.

Methodism through all of its history has had a center of authority for the governing of the denomination. Following Wesley's death British Methodism found its center in the British Conference, which met annually. In the United States the newly independent Methodist Episcopal Church looked to the General Conference for its center of authority, a practice that is still followed. The General Conference is a representative group of clergy and laypeople who meet every four years. In the debate about what The United Methodist Church's position on a particular issue may be, the phrase is still heard, "Only the General Conference can speak for The United Methodist Church." The importance given the General Conference is a recognition that it is still the tangible authority.

Over the course of the years the structure, beliefs, and organization of the denomination have changed drastically. United Methodism has gone through schisms and mergers. It has become a large and highly diverse American denomination. Nevertheless, it still perceives itself to be a connectional system and believes that this is one of its unique aspects.

Two Aspects of Connectionalism

There are two distinct aspects of the United Methodist connectional system or two kinds of glue holding the denomination together. The first is the commitment that both clergy and laity have to the connectional system.

They believe that this system is a good, if not the best, way for the denomination to be structured. Because United Methodists share this belief, they act in ways that help insure the continuance of the connection.

When an individual joins a local United Methodist church he or she is considered to be a member of the total connection. This is explicitly stated in the *Discipline,* "A member of any local United Methodist church is a member of the total United Methodist connection" (Paragraph 210). It is the denomination, through the General Conference, that sets the standards for membership and prescribes the manner by which persons will be received into the church. However, the local congregation, or more specifically the pastor, has a great deal of flexibility in determining how these standards are interpreted.

The connectional system assumes that the members agree to be subject to the discipline of their church. In the early days the standards of discipline were strictly enforced; persons who neglected their responsibilities or vows were subject to reprimand and even expulsion from the fellowship. While there is still provision for a trial, which could lead to the expulsion of a member from the church, such an event seldom occurs. An occasional member of the clergy may be dismissed from the ministry; the termination of a layperson's membership in The United Methodist Church is so rare as to be virtually nonexistent. Church members today set their own standards for Christian living with the result that there is a wide range in what is accepted as appropriate behavior for United Methodists. The church offers guidance but no longer insists on adherence to specific rules.

While adherence to the United Methodist connectional system is voluntary, there are certain requirements that tie the local church very closely to the parent denomination. These requirements provide the second type of glue that holds the connection together.

The organization of every local church is determined not by that congregation but by the General Conference. This makes a specific congregational structure mandatory, which, like one size of a ready-made suit designed for the average man, hardly fits anyone exactly.

An important link in the official structure that ties the local church to the denomination has been and continues to be the district superintendent. In fact, district superintendents and bishops are considered to be "ministers" of each local congregation within their jurisdiction. It is therefore proper for them to interject themselves into the affairs of a congregation; they in fact have responsibility for each local church.

Another important aspect is the requirement that the district superintendent (or an ordained elder appointed to act in his behalf) preside over the Charge Conference or the annual business meeting of the local church. Thus when the important policy, budgetary, and administrative decisions are made by the congregation, the presiding officer is not a locally elected layperson or the pastor but the district superintendent, the representative of the denomination. The relationship of the congregation to the larger denomination and its membership in a connectional system is made clear by the district superintendent chairing the Charge Conferences.

As has already been pointed out, pastors of United Methodist churches are appointed by the bishop with the local people having only an advisory role. The conditions that a congregation must meet to secure a pastor are determined not by the congregation itself but by the Annual Conference. These include the required minimum salary, a parsonage that meets certain standards, and other benefits for the clergy. The local church is made aware that it is a part of a larger body when the time comes for securing a minister.

A final way that the local church is tied closely into the connectional system is by the restrictions on its property. The *Discipline* states that The United Methodist Church is organized as a connectional church and titles to all properties shall be held in trust for The United Methodist Church. All deeds of United Methodist churches are to contain a trust clause that states, in part: *"In trust, that said premises shall be used, kept, and maintained as a place of divine worship of the United Methodist ministry and members of The United Methodist Church; subject to the Discipline, usage, and ministerial appointments of said church"* (Paragraph 2503).

This paragraph protects the United Methodist people (and the denomination) from a dissident group within the local church that might want to withdraw from the denomination and take control of the property. Thus a local congregation by a vote of 51 percent of the members cannot simply withdraw from The United Methodist Church. Individual members may leave but they cannot go as a congregation and continue to hold title to the property.

Thus, when property is purchased or given to The United Methodist Church, its use is reserved for the purpose for which it was purchased or given. A local church can of course sell property but to do so it must have the approval of the district superintendent. If a church is abandoned, the property goes to the Annual Conference, which may dispose of it and use the proceeds to invest in other church property. Once an investment is made in United Methodist church property it can never be lost. Should it become impractical for a church to exist at one location, the assets can be transferred to another place to carry on the ministry of the church.

Another visible and legal aspect of connectionalism is found in the District Board of Church Location and Building. This board, which is required in each district, investigates every proposed local church building site and determines whether it is an appropriate site on which to establish a United Methodist church. This group may take into consideration the possible effect of a proposed new or relocated congregation on other United Methodist churches in the area. This board also must give its approval to a local church wishing to purchase or construct a new building or parsonage or remodel its building if the cost is to exceed 10 percent of the present value. The result is to require each congregation, whenever it is either erecting a new building or doing extensive remodeling, to have the approval of an outside group. This clearly emphasizes the place of the congregation in the connection and the mutual responsibility that United Methodist churches are expected to have for one another.

The relationship between a local church and the denomination is a complex arrangement of rights and obligations, powers and duties. The congregation is expected to be loyal to the denomination, to accept the pastor the bishop appoints, and to pay its fair share of the money requested for the administration of the denomination and for its benevolent and mission enterprises. The denomination in turn is expected to provide a pastor, resources, and program materials and to supervise the work of the pastor and the ministry of the local church.

Some degree of tension can be expected between local churches and the denomination. First, the denomination expects the congregation to contribute funds to cover the administrative costs and support various benevolent programs. There will always be some persons who feel that a larger portion of these funds should remain in the local church. Furthermore the denomination may want the local church to participate in certain programs, a statewide evangelistic crusade for instance. These will be resisted by some congregations. Denominational agencies may support causes that some congregations disapprove. These result in tension between the two.

The belief in the connectional system has tended to make the whole (the denomination) greater than the sum of its parts (the local churches). This concept is strengthened by the clergy who frequently appeal to the authority of the denomination as a way of achieving some goal within the local church, a goal that may be in conflict with the desires of persons in the congregation. In the final analysis, however, the greater power rests with the congregation. While the denominational structures have authority in some areas, their power to exercise this authority is dependent on the willingness of the local church to accept their actions as legitimate. For example, while a bishop makes the decision as to which pastor shall be appointed, the congregation must be willing to have that individual serve as pastor and to provide the necessary salary and benefits. The argument may be raised that a local church and its members must in fact accede to the denominational rules if they are to be United Methodists. This is of course true, but no one is required to be a member of The United Methodist Church. Furthermore there is no assurance that any particular denomination, not to mention its effective functioning, depends on mutual trust and accountability between the various parts of the organization. These include the local churches, the Annual Conferences, and the various general boards, agencies, and institutions.

While there will always be some level of tension within a social institution as large and as diverse as The United Methodist Church, for the institution to survive there must be a minimal level of consensus concerning the goals and methods appropriate for that body. The increasing number of organized caucus groups whose avowed purpose is to control the denomination (or at least certain parts of it) for their specific agenda does not bode well for the future of the connectional system. The denomination will in all probability survive, but certain aspects of connectionalism could become casualties. Other denominations which are associations of autonomous congregations have long existed and prospered also. If United Methodism becomes more pluralistic and congregations sense a greater degree of estrangement from the total denomination, the result could be a weakening of the connectional ideology and an increasing willingness to view the denomination as a looser federation of local churches.

Maintaining the Connection

Maintaining an ideology that results in an appreciation of and a loyalty to the denomination is an ongoing task. Children must learn what their church believes and how it operates; they need to understand its distinctive role in the larger Christian community. New members must also be socialized into the United Methodist system. This is a continuing task because there is a constant inflow of persons from churches of others denominations. In a recent four-year period, 17 percent of the persons who were received into membership of The United Methodist Church came by transfer from churches of other denominations. Some 45 percent of the new members joined by confession of faith; included in this group were children who completed the confirmation class. Therefore, a substantial number of United Methodist members have little or no background in the United Methodist denomination. Given the minimal emphasis that goes into membership training in most local churches, it should not be surprising that appreciation of United Methodism is not greater among the laity.

Some of the reluctance to emphasize denominational distinctiveness and the need for loyalty has been due to the ecumenical movement of the past half century. The assumptions that denominations are the result of human sinfulness and that a truly Christian church would be unified are rarely challenged. The assumption that the various denominations are gradually evolving into one has also been generally accepted, despite evidence to the contrary. It appears that many clergy feel a bit guilty if they point out the unique characteristics and contributions of their denomination. The long-term effect may be to weaken the average layperson's loyalty to the denomination without making a corresponding contribution to the unification of Christianity.

Denominations are essential to the local church. They fulfill an essential social function for the congregation. They provide a kind of brand name that identifies what goes on in a local church. The individual who sees a church building with a sign labeling it a "United Presbyterian Church" will have some understanding of the beliefs of the members, and the nature of the services conducted. He or she would certainly know that a United Presbyterian Church is different from one with a sign reading "Fire Baptized Holiness Church."

The denomination provides a wide variety of services for the local churches. These range from assistance in securing a pastor to the production of literature for use in the church school. A major function of the denomination has been to provide resources to enable the local congregation to function more effectively. Denominational agencies also carry out mission projects in behalf of their constituency, activities which the local church supports but which are beyond its individual capabilities.

A net result of United Methodist connectionalism has been to tie the local churches into the larger denominational system. For the average layperson this is manifest in loyalty to the denomination, a loyalty that in fact does more to provide cohesion than do the restrictions related to church property.

There are certain advantages to a connectional system. It helps the individual feel part of the larger Christian community, or at least that represented by the parent denomination. It helps the local congregation and the individual members feel a responsibility for the larger mission of the church.

The connectional system's most significant advantage is that it protects the interests of the total denomination against unfriendly or precipitous action by local groups. A local church cannot simply withdraw from the denomination and retain the property. The building remains in the custody of the righteous remnant, even if they are a minority of loyal United Methodists.

The United Methodist connectional system has stressed the unity of the entire denomination and the accountability of the various parts to one another. Like any other form of church polity, it has strengths and weaknesses and like other church organizations it has been experiencing some strains and undergoing some changes. Nevertheless, it continues to provide both a theoretical framework and a practical method for relating the local churches to the denomination and to one another and will continue to do so as the denomination enters its third century.

CHAPTER 8

Power and Authority in the Local Church

In the 1970s the church developed a great interest in the concepts of power and authority.[1] As membership has declined and institutional strength has waned, more persons seem to be spending time and energy trying to gain a greater degree of control over the denominational structure and its related institutions and agencies. Probably at no time in the history of United Methodism have there been more organized caucus groups, representing persons differentiated by sex, age, ethnicity, social goals, and theological beliefs. All of these are attempting to exercise power within the denomination to achieve group or personal objectives.

While the struggle for power continues, the denomination seems to be undergoing a crisis of authority. There is no agreement on what is the legitimate authority for the church. The bottom line has become how to make events happen and people act. Power, even in a religious organization, can become exploitive when the common authority for the church and its ministry is lost. The popularization of power can in part be explained as a result of the loss of a transcendent common authority that binds people together. When this occurs we look to new voices; we are told how to win through intimidation and that we should be looking out for number one. The

United Methodist Church has its transcendent authority—the fourfold Wesleyan quadrilateral: Scripture, tradition, reason, and experience. These have lost their appeal to many in the church and with it their power. The result is a search for authority and power that will insure the survival of the institution and provide at least tentative solutions to the most pressing problems. Controlling the institution comes to be the primary goal; this, it is assumed, will result in a multitude of unidentified desirable ends.

The theological problem with the popular gravitation toward power is that it is essentially narcissistic. It is not only self-centered, it is destructively self-centered because there is no motivation for moving toward participation by the whole group, for establishing group loyalties, or for giving up personal objectives to achieve those of the entire group. The problem is not that learning how to attain and use power is wrong, but that the dynamics of individual control and corporate manipulation are not related to the larger community and the transcendent authorities: the Bible, the creeds, and the traditions of church life.

The concern for power and its use in the church can be found at all levels of the church. It is particularly prevalent among those church leaders whose major interest is the operation of the denomination. This would include the professional administrators and other clergy and laypersons who hold denominational offices. It is probably safe to assume that the overwhelming majority of members of local churches are more concerned about the life and ministry of their congregation. What the national church does is judged in terms of its positive or negative effect on the local congregation. Congregations have a life of their own, which of course is only partially determined by the denomination.

Authority in the Congregation

In the previous chapter the nature of the United Methodist connectional system and its impact on the local churches were considered. No Protestant denomination has greater authority over the local church than does The United Methodist Church. This is exercised through the appointment of the pastor, the supervision of the district superintendent, and the required local church organization. It should be noted that these items all deal with the operation of the local church as a social organization; none is related to the tenets of the faith. Although there is a body of doctrine that is associated with United Methodism, there is no insistence that lay members adhere to all of it. There is an increasing strictness regarding the theological beliefs held by candidates for the ministry, but this seems more related to an oversupply of clergy necessitating the rejection of some applicants than to a renewed interest in theology.

When it comes to matters of the content of the Christian faith and its implication for an appropriate life-style, the local churches and the individuals are left on their own. What United Methodists believe about the inspiration of the Scriptures, for example, is left up to each member to decide. The denomination provides guidelines but there is no definitive statement concerning the official position. The result is that within the denomination a wide range of beliefs will be found.

Where do church members acquire their beliefs? There is no clear answer other than by the socialization process within the congregation by which the individuals are taught the faith. This would include church school classes, sermons, youth groups, revival meetings, church camps, and the interaction with other members of the congregation over a period of years. As a result, different local churches develop different theological traditions, which range from those that could be described as liberal to some that are very conservative, with the majority falling somewhere in between these two extremes.

The pastor tends to have considerable influence on the theological stance of a congregation. This is particularly true if a pastor has served an unusually long term or if a church has had several pastors with similar theological viewpoints. Such ministers tend to attract people who share these beliefs; they also persuade persons to accept their way of thinking. The result is that over a period of time a congregation may develop a kind of theological consensus that becomes the norm for that church. The local congregation then becomes their own source of authority although they would be quick to insist that such a source was outside the group and found in the Scriptures, the traditions of the church, and so forth.

Once a congregation develops a theological identity, it can come into conflict with the appointive power of the bishop. The members may insist on a pastor who holds beliefs compatible with the congregation's. The bishop may be unwilling to provide the type of pastor desired; he may want to send in a pastor who as one district superintendent observed, "Will bring that church back into the mainstream of Methodism." Only those churches on the theological extremes seem to develop a clear theological identity.

As with theological beliefs, determining what is appropriate Christian conduct is increasingly left up to the individual with some guidance from the denomination. The amount and clarity of such guidance has been decreasing so that in this area the local congregation is

left more and more on its own. As the denominational
boards and agencies have given greater emphasis to more
generalized societal problems, less attention has been
given to matters of individual morality and Christian
standards of conduct. In some instances the agencies
have been working for less strict standards for church
members, despite the opposition from some of their
constituents who still support traditional United Methodist requirements.

United Methodism has had a tradition of keeping one
major sin before its constituents and designing appropriate national agencies to accomplish this task. For many
years a major United Methodist concern was the
consumption of beverage alcohol. The church's position
on this subject was clear; it was total abstinence. The
misnamed Board of Temperance was set up to promote
this cause. The Board of Temperance has long since been
combined with other agencies, and although alcohol is a
major problem in society today, the United Methodist
position on the subject is not presented with the strength
it was half a century ago. Now United Methodism is
concerned about another sin, racism in its many forms.
The Commission on Religion and Race has been
established to deal with it.

Power of the Congregation

Local churches and United Methodist members accept
the authority of the denomination because they believe
that such authority is valid. The denomination can exist
only because the local people are willing participants in
the system by giving their approval and with it their time
and money. Church members believe in their church and
its leaders. They in fact want to believe in the wisdom and
effectiveness of their denomination. To fail to do so

would be a negative reflection on themselves, because they know they are providing the resources that make the existence of the denomination possible. This is why legitimate criticism may be met with disbelief and even hostility. People do not like to be told that a group in which they have put both their trust and money has been unfaithful or devious, even if this is true.

A local United Methodist church has veto power over many denominational activities as they affect that particular congregation. To participate in a denominational activity or to support a benevolent cause or not to do so is within the power of the local church. The connectional system that stresses the importance of the entire church reminds the congregation that loyal United Methodists put the needs of the total church ahead of the local group. Requests come to the congregation with the clear expectation that the response will be positive.

The *Discipline* prescribes the types of internal organization that a local church must have. The formal structure is designed to meet two different goals. The first is to provide an organization that will provide for the various functions of the local church. There is a Board of Trustees responsible for property, a Finance Committee to see that the budget is raised, a work area on education to provide for Christian nurture, and so forth. These are all legitimate aspects of the local church. The second goal is to provide a unit in the congregation that parallels the various boards and agencies and to provide these organizations with a volunteer representative on the local level. This is one reason why the number of required official positions and organizations in the local church has increased so greatly in recent years.

Most congregations dutifully elect persons to fill all the required positions and organizations. In some small churches there will be much overlapping but the letter of the law is usually fulfilled. A name is turned in on the appropriate Charge Conference form and someone is added to a mailing list in some board or agency office.

The local church is a stable and durable institution. The people know, whether they verbalize it or not, that what is important is that their church is effective, that it is a place where the Word is preached and the sacraments administered, and that its members form a caring and loving community. They see the stability of the local church as a virtue, a symbol, which links the present congregation to both the "great cloud of witnesses" that have gone before and to the Kingdom that will be realized in the future.

Local Decision-Making

In the normal course of a congregation's operation many decisions must be made. In the regulations regarding the local church in the *Discipline* the authority of the pastor, the congregational officials, and the various committees is clearly stated. However, the decision-making process is affected by factors other than the procedures stated in the bylaws.

When Methodism was a collection of classes under the direction of a leader, the decision-making process was clear. The leader operated under rules set forth by John Wesley and the group exercised discipline over its members. As the number of churches increased, and as congregations grew in size, more complex formal organizational patterns were developed until we now have the present structure.

There are two factors to note in considering the internal organization of local United Methodist churches. First, the way the congregation operates is dependent upon its size. A church with a very small membership (one of under a hundred) will be very informal. The active members will tend to participate in the major decisions. Certain laypersons or families may have an unusual amount of influence. There may even be one individual who is a kind of church boss, a person who may not even hold any elected office, but who has the respect of the congregation. The members may defer to this person and follow his or her advice when decisions are to be made. This informal process can cut across the formal lines of authority so that matters are not handled in the proper channels. This can be very frustrating for the pastor and the district superintendent who are not a part of this informal system. The decision may be made at a church meeting when the pastor is not present, or it may even be made at a gathering away from the church.

One pastor who serves a three-point circuit described one of the churches operating in an informal manner:

> The people at Mt. Bethel Church seem to be able to do anything they want. They listen to my suggestions but make up their own minds. Last February I arrived for the Sunday service and discovered that they had painted the sanctuary. They take good care of their church so I don't have to be concerned about it.

As a church increases in size, the governing procedures necessarily become more formal. This is necessary because the group is too large for decisions to be made on an *ad hoc* basis. Authority and responsibility for specific areas of the congregational life must be delegated. The congregation becomes more segmented as persons gravitate to areas because of interests or friendships or a combination of both. The pastor occupies a critical role in the larger churches. The large churches are more dependent on the pastor to provide direction. As a kind of executive officer, the minister of the large congregation may exercise more power than the pastor of a church of small membership. Lyle E. Schaller, who has analyzed the issues regarding the staffs of large churches, says, "Larger congregations tend to be more impersonal, to emphasize the functional aspects of the church rather than to undergird the relational dimensions of congregational life, to place greater demands on the staff in general and on the senior minister in particular."[2]

The second factor is the gradual increase in the power of laypersons in both the denomination and the local church. As has been pointed out, Methodism has been and continues to be a church in which the clergy are dominant. However, over the long term the trend has been for the laity to acquire more power. This trend is continuing and the long-term prospect is for the laity to exercise even greater power. The required consultation with the local church regarding the appointment of the pastor is just one indicator; the breaking down of the itineracy system as evidenced by permitting clergy to serve part-time is another. To rebel against systems that are perceived as authoritarian is part of a trend in the larger society. This will continue to be an issue as The United Methodist Church enters its third century.

CHAPTER 9

United Methodism's Minorities

United Methodism has never been a denomination with a membership limited only to persons of one racial or cultural group. From the earliest days of the church in America, there have been members and congregations other than white and/or English-speaking. The number and proportion of United Methodism's minority membership has varied over the years. As the denomination enters its third century the number of racial and non-English language minority constituencies constitute somewhat less than 5 percent of the total membership.

Each ethnic and language minority constitutes a social subsystem within the denomination. This chapter will consider the way the ethnic and language groups function within the denomination, the relationship of the minority churches to other congregations, and the current trends in the relationship of the minorities to the total church.

Black United Methodists

The largest minority within The United Methodist Church is its black members.[1] Blacks have been a part of the denomination during virtually all its history in America. It is reported that John Wesley baptized his first

Negro converts in Wandsworth, England, on November 29, 1758. Early black preachers included Harry Hosier, Henry Evans, and John Stewart. Harry Hosier, known as Black Harry, was a gifted preacher who accompanied Francis Asbury on many of his missions. In the period before the Civil War, names of blacks were found on the rolls of some congregations in the South, although the presence of slave galleries in some of the old churches attests to their status in both church and society. In the North various ministries were undertaken for the Negro residents. The African Methodist Episcopal Church was established by black members who withdrew from the Methodist Episcopal Church.

The conclusion of the Civil War led to two significant developments. First, the Methodist Episcopal Church, South, assisted in the formation of the Colored Methodist Episcopal Church (later changed to Christian Methodist Episcopal) by former slaves. The M.E. Church, South, continued to provide financial support to certain of the C.M.E. institutions, a practice that is still carried on by The United Methodist Church. Second, the northern Methodist Episcopal Church sent missionaries to the South after the Civil War to evangelize the freedmen and organize them into congregations. Thus from reconstruction until the unification of the three branches of Methodism in 1939, there were hundreds of black Methodist Episcopal congregations affiliated with northern Methodism located in the states that had made up the Confederacy.

A major difficulty confronting the persons attempting to bring about the merger of the three branches of Methodism in the late 1930s was what to do with the black churches and Annual Conferences in the still segregated South; the merger of the white and black Annual Conferences was not considered an option at that time.

This issue had contributed to the failure of negotiations a decade earlier. A compromise was reached and the Central Jurisdiction was established. The country was divided into five geographic regions called jurisdictions, which elected bishops and members of the boards of the national church agencies. The Annual Conferences in these five regional jurisdictions consisted of white congregations. The West Coast was an exception; here the Japanese Provisional Conference was part of the Western Jurisdiction and some black and other ethnic and language congregations were part of predominantly white Annual Conferences. Most black churches were grouped into the Central Jurisdiction, which overlapped the others. This insured that there would be black bishops and black representatives on the boards of managers of the national church agencies. However, it left the denomination with a segregated structure that was the subject of intense debate until it was abolished at the time of the merger with the Evangelical United Brethren denomination over a quarter of a century later.

The Central Jurisdiction made up a subsystem of Annual Conferences and local churches for black Methodists. It was a kind of church within a church, which provided that blacks would be represented at the national church level and assured them that they would have control over their segment of the denomination. It was Methodism's version of the separate-but-equal concept. Like all segregated structures there was little contact between the parts. Black and white Methodist churches in the same city were under the supervision of different district superintendents and bishops, participated in different events, and had virtually no contact with one another. The writer recalls interviewing two Methodist pastors in a southern city in 1964. Although their churches and parsonages were only three and a half blocks apart and both had been there for more than four years, these ministers had never met.

The Central Jurisdiction was a segregated structure and was increasingly viewed as unacceptable by both black and white Methodists. Furthermore, the black membership was declining. Most of the congregations were in the South; thirteen of the seventeen black Annual Conferences were in the states that had made up the Confederacy. A large number of blacks was moving to the North and Methodism was having only limited success winning members among the increasing numbers of urban blacks. It was with a sigh of relief that the denomination approved a plan to end the Central Jurisdiction and merge the black and white conferences.

The end of the Central Jurisdiction has meant the loss of power by the black United Methodists except as it is granted by the white majority. The election of a black bishop, for example, is now dependent on the votes of the predominantly white jurisdictional conference delegates. Affirmative action sentiment is strong in the denomination so an attempt is made to see that all minorities are represented at all levels of the church. In fact, the proportion of minority persons related to the national agencies as board and staff members is far greater than the proportion of minorities in the United Methodist constituency.

On the local level a large majority of blacks are members of all-black congregations. While there are more black members in predominantly white local churches than is generally assumed, the principle of congregational homogeneity applies; people select churches in which they feel comfortable and where they find the experience meaningful. In this regard, black church members function in the same way as whites; they select a church that meets their needs. Furthermore, the emphasis on a distinctive black style of religion will assure the continuance of all-black congregations for the indefinite future.

The discontinuance of a formal, all-black organizational structure has resulted in an informal one. Black pastors tend to be appointed to black churches; black representation in denominational positions is arranged by the church leadership. In fact, black representation at the General Conference has been at an all time high as each Annual Conference is careful to include some black members on their delegation although the black proportion of a conference's membership may be very small. The Black Methodists for Church Renewal is an organization that provides a national forum for blacks. Caucus groups keep black concerns before the Annual Conferences. These provide some of the functions previously carried on by the Central Jurisdiction.

While the black presence is clearly visible in the national church and in the general boards and agencies, the evidence is that the black local churches are decreasing. Many of the black local churches are located in rural areas of the South where the population has been declining. Only a very small proportion of the black population of the large cities is United Methodist. Despite an adequate supply of clergy generally, finding black pastors for the black local churches is a problem.

The concern of the denomination for black churches is evidenced by the funds being expended by the national church on black projects and churches. The Ethnic Minority Local Church Fund adopted in 1976 is the latest such effort and is in addition to the sums already being provided by the national agencies and Annual Conferences. Unfortunately, subsidies by the denomination may have an effect opposite to what is hoped. Such funds may make the clergy and the local churches more dependent on outside support so that the congregation will not be required to build their support in the communities in which they are located. When subsidies produce dependency, the result is weaker local churches. One black church leader has written: "The black church has too long been the object of mission. Many of our churches have been crippled by the welfare system of the Board of Mission and Church Extension. Total dependence upon this system of support in some instances stifles the creativity of their programs."[2]

The continuation of a black United Methodist constituency will depend on the ability of the black churches to develop strong congregations supported by their members. It is still uncertain whether ethnic identity and customs can be preserved in a predominantly white denomination, at least to the degree that the members of minorities desire. At this point it is also uncertain whether the black local United Methodist church can win a sufficient number of persons to assure that there will continue to be a black presence within the denomination. The early years of Methodism's third century will be crucial in this.

Cultural Minorities

As United Methodism enters its third century many of its members may not be aware that their denomination has within its background many cultural groups. As the United States received large numbers of immigrants, Methodism responded by helping these persons establish churches and in some cases Annual Conferences. There have been Methodist churches where the principle language spoken was Italian, Swedish, Norwegian, Danish, German, Chinese, Japanese, Bohemian, Polish, and Spanish. There have been Annual Conferences made up of such language groups as: Norwegian, Danish, German, Japanese, and Chinese. While these Annual Conferences have ceased to exist, there are still two conferences that serve a language or ethnic group; the Rio Grande (Spanish) and the Oklahoma Indian.

In order for a cultural group to have congregations or an Annual Conference over a continuing period of time, it must have both a sufficiently large group and a continuing influx of people. The process of acculturation has resulted in most of the non-English language churches eventually being discontinued. The pattern has been for the non-English speaking church to continue for a generation until the immigrant generation passed from the scene. Eventually the church either became an English-speaking congregation, little different from others of the denomination, or it closed. The exceptions are the Spanish-speaking congregations that can continue because of the continued immigration of large numbers of persons whose native language is Spanish. A similar pattern on a smaller scale can be noted in the increase in congregations consisting of several Asian groups. The arrival of immigrants from Asia provides a constituency for these churches.

A fundamental difference may exist between the earlier period and today. During the time when large numbers of Europeans were migrating to the United States, it was assumed that they would be acculturated into the mainstream of American life. While groups tried to teach their children their native language, the public schools taught in English. The pattern for the children of immigrants was to reject the customs of the parents and become highly Americanized. The next generation or the grandchildren tended to be far enough removed from the immigrant families' insecurities to affirm their heritage and be Polish-Americans or German-Americans.

The non-English church was a bastion of the immigrants' culture, a place where they could preserve some of the familiar ways of the home country.

The present situation differs from earlier periods in one significant way. Then, the assumption was that the immigrant was in due course going to fit into the American way of life; now the official policy is to attempt to preserve the multitude of cultural heritages. For example, the public schools today are mandated to teach in the immigrants' language. It is uncertain whether the present policies will retard participation of the new arrivals in the mainstream of American life by helping create cultural ghettos. However, the forces of acculturation are such that even the government programs, such as school instruction in other than English, probably will not keep the immigrant cultural group and language intact beyond the first generation unless there continues to be a substantial number of new arrivals.

Another factor in the current scene is the attitude of the member of the ethnic or cultural group. If the individual wants to move into what is perceived as the mainstream of American life, membership in a church of a major denomination may contribute to attaining that goal. Such church membership may lead to participation in other aspects of the denomination and provide contacts with a variety of persons outside the limited cultural group. On the other hand, if persons are content to find their primary identity in the ethnic or cultural group, they may be more likely to join a church consisting of members of that group. The ethnic has the option of joining a predominantly white congregation, an ethnic local church affiliated with a predominantly white denomination such as United Methodist, or an ethnic congregation affiliated with a denomination made up predominantly of churches with the same cultural heritage. The ethnic who has a strong appreciation for ethnic culture and religion may be inclined to join a church of an all-ethnic denomination rather than one affiliated with a predominantly white denomination.

Conflicting Goals

A fundamental strategic issue that United Methodism has not yet resolved is whether the ethnic and/or non-English congregation is intended as only an instrument for bringing the Christian message to the members of a particular group or whether its purpose includes the preservation of a particular culture and language. In an earlier time the answer would have been clear. The non-English-speaking congregation was organized so persons could hear the gospel and be saved.

Today the church seems to be attempting to affirm and maintain the various subcultures while at the same time claiming a commitment to an ideal of inclusiveness. These two goals appear to be contradictory. In this regard the church finds itself in the same dilemma as the large society.

The decision that the denomination must sooner or later make is whether the goal is to make the church as inclusive as possible or to accept the various ethnic and cultural subsystems as inevitable and permanent parts of United Methodism. Such a decision will be the result of a variety of social forces and a multitude of decisions and actions at all levels of the church. It will depend on how United Methodist people perceive the nature of their church and the relationship of persons of different ethnic and cultural groups within the denomination. The final result will determine not only the role of minority members within the denomination but also the number of minority members within United Methodism.

CHAPTER 10

Issues for the Third Century

Local United Methodist churches and the denomination are the result of a combination of factors: the theology of the members, the shared traditions, the contemporary society, and the actions of church leaders at critical times in the history of the church. Indeed, the type of church that exists today owes much to the decisions of those who preceded us. The church of fifty or a hundred years from now will in part be shaped by what is done today.

This final chapter will consider some of the issues that confront United Methodism as it enters its third century. This is not a chapter that will attempt to predict the future; such an exercise would be futile because our guesses would in all probability be incorrect. Instead this chapter will focus on those factors that are already upon us, issues that require immediate decisions and actions. These are matters with which we as United Methodists must deal, not in twenty-five or fifty years but tomorrow and the day after. How we deal or fail to deal with these issues will determine what United Methodism will be like in its third century.

Theological Clarity

As United Methodism enters its third century there is neither clarity nor consensus about its basic theology.

While the denomination never has had a rigid belief system, there has been a kind of accepted theological core that has been identified with United Methodism. In this period of our history there seems to be less agreement on what is the common theology that holds the church together.

It is not the purpose of this book to consider what the content of this theology should be, but to examine what the consequences of a lack of theological clarity may be for the local church as a social institution. The ideology of a group helps provide a sense of identity, a series of common goals, and an acceptable style of group life. Because of what we believe about God, we do certain things (i.e., join a local church, attend worship, contribute to the fund to feed the hungry) and refrain from doing certain things (i.e., swearing, being unpleasant to neighbors). If the theology held by the members of a group is diverse, their actions will also differ and conflict can be the result.

United Methodism has always been pluralistic although it has only recently begun to use that term. A range of beliefs and practices has been acceptable but the unity of the denomination was stressed. One of the bishops once compared Methodism to a three-ring circus. While there were different things going on in each of the rings, all were united under the big tent of the denomination.

The acceptance of pluralism as a positive characteristic of the church does not mean that every type of theology will be acceptable. As this term seems to be used, it describes the range of acceptable beliefs and actions that the denomination will tolerate. Pluralism does have its boundaries. Having accepted pluralism, these boundaries will now have to be more clearly defined. Probably this will not be done in a formal way, but the limits of

pluralism will be tested and defined as persons on the
extreme ends of the liberal and conservative spectrum
discover, to their discomfort, that they have passed the
point where an acceptable United Methodist position ends.
To push the circus analogy a bit farther, the denomination
will have to determine what can occur under United
Methodism's big top and what will be relegated to the freak
side shows that must remain outside.

Some theological clarity is essential to maintaining an
identity and unity. This can emerge only as the
denomination at all levels gives more attention to
theology. It cannot be delegated to a general committee
of experts although such groups have a significant
contribution to make. Whatever theological consensus
may develop within, United Methodism will emerge
from the life of the church as the people struggle with the
message and demands of the gospel in the world of today.

Faith and Pessimism

The statement is often made that The United
Methodist Church is experiencing a failure of nerve, that
a sense of pessimism exists throughout the denomination. There seems to be no doubt that this is an accurate
description of some of the leaders of the church. A recent
study of the opinions of denominational leaders concerning the present state and future course of United
Methodism by Alan K. Waltz, a research specialist of the
General Council on Ministries, confirms this gloomy
outlook. "The picture . . . seems to be of a denomination
primarily concerned with administering its past and
describing the symptoms of its present malaise, but
unwilling to seek a better understanding of its discomfort
or to take the requisite steps to effect a cure."[1] The
persons surveyed indicated that one of the most pressing

needs was for The United Methodist Church to develop a clear sense of purpose and unity for its life and work, but they were not optimistic that this would be accomplished.

The high degree of pessimism among denominational leaders is having its effect on local churches, particularly on the clergy. As part of a study of the urban church, I interviewed a pastor in a midwestern city. The church was not one of the denomination's prestige pulpits; it had an average congregation in a residential neighborhood, a place where people raise their families and attempt to make sense out of life. As I entered the minister's study and introduced myself, he greeted me with, "You must find your job discouraging the way the church is failing everywhere."

There is, of course, much vitality in the local churches. Often the vitality and optimistic spirit present in local churches is in sharp contrast to the pessimism prevalent in the other levels of the denomination. The congregation fortunately is somewhat isolated from the rest of the denomination; it is affected mainly by what is happening in the local community and within the congregation. If the pastor has a deep faith and is committed to sharing this with the people, if the congregation is a loving and caring group, the local church will be alive and the people confident and optimistic.

The Christian faith that has the Resurrection as a central tenet can never be pessimistic. Rupert E. Davies writes that a fundamental aspect of Methodism is the "insistence that the heart of Christianity lies in the personal commerce of a man with his Lord, who has saved him and won the forgiveness of his sins, and will live in him to transform his character."[2] Such a faith inspires confidence and optimism.

Why does the high level of pessimism exist within United Methodism? One possible explanation might lie in the goals toward which the church has worked in the past quarter of a century. Increasingly the objectives have been defined in social and economic terms; it was assumed that personal faith and commitment would somehow occur. While these causes may be worthwhile, there are two factors that may contribute to the prevailing pessimism. First, many of the societal problems to which the church has officially addressed itself and committed substantial sums of money are exceedingly complex and defy easy or immediate solutions. Poverty is one example; world hunger is another. These are critical issues but defy solutions except over a very long period of time, probably across several generations. Second, the goals are essentially secular and are devoid of any transcendent aspect. Even when they are successful, they do not result in any sense of joy and accomplishment but only call attention to the many other evils and injustices in the society that need correcting. A boycott that causes a company to have better labor practices, or results in a bank discontinuing loans in South Africa hardly brings the church a sense of triumph that the kingdom of God is closer. Lose or win, there is a transient quality about secular objectives that can produce a sense of frustration and contribute to the climate of pessimism. The situation will not be changed by increased efforts.

A change in the outlook of United Methodism can only come through a renewal of faith by persons at all levels of the church. Such is more likely to occur by an emphasis on theology, on the biblical basis of the Christian faith, and on greater attention to the traditions of United Methodism. All this will be of little importance without the consideration of another of the characteristics of United Methodism as stated by Rupert E. Davies, a "stress on the doctrine of the Holy Spirit, the Person of the Trinity who is often neglected by institutional Christianity, yet without whom neither the fulfilment of the Lord's commandments nor the common life of the Christian community is more than a vague aspiration."[3]

The Membership Decline

The factor that gives the most dramatic evidence of the state of United Methodism is the decrease in membership of the past decade and a half. The harsh fact is that substantially fewer persons are joining the churches. Should this trend continue, the implications will be enormous for every aspect of denominational life.

For the past quarter of a century the denomination has emphasized broad societal and churchwide goals. The most significant ministries were perceived to be those outside the church. The world was to set the agenda for the church to follow. The congregation that was perceived to be really in ministry was doing something in the community, starting a day care center, having an emergency relief program, or mounting a campaign for some social cause. The message was clear that the traditional activities such as worship, Bible study, prayer groups were of lesser importance. Pastors of churches that were experiencing an increase in membership were made to feel that they were not being faithful to the gospel. Through all this period there was the assumption that people would somehow automatically continue to become Christians, join the church, and support the programs and missional activities of the denomination.

United Methodism must now reexamine the role of the church in society and the meaning of church membership. It seems clear that people are not coming into the church to provide support troops for the denominational programs. It may be time to realize again that the major function of the Christian community is *to be* rather than *to do*. As United Methodism enters its third century it may discover that its product is after all religion, clarifying the relationship of men and women to God, understanding sin, finding forgiveness, and defining the transcendent values that give meaning and purpose to life. If this occurs, more persons may perceive the church as an institution worthy of their allegiance, their time, and their substance.

The Impact of Structure

A significant but somewhat lesser issue is the influence that the denominational structure has on the local church. The trend in recent years has been for the general church agencies to have a life of their own, which may have a negative influence on the local churches. It has already been pointed out that the local church organization is in part designed to provide the general agencies with local representatives. This may or may not be helpful or appropriate for a particular congregation.

While United Methodism has had and now affirms theological pluralism, it has insisted upon a high degree of organizational conformity. While there is some flexibility for congregations of small membership, all local churches are required to be organized in the approved manner. If there is any action that is clearly a heresy in The United Methodist Church, it is to deviate from the official organization as set forth in the *Discipline*.

A trend in recent years has been to tinker continually with the denominational machinery. While it is necessary to alter the church organization to meet new conditions in the larger society, many of the changes seem to have been primarily cosmetic. The urgency to change the structure has been in part the result of a sense of uncertainty concerning what the church should be about, combined with the feeling that something must be done.

In such a situation, the easiest thing (and probably the least productive) is to make alterations in the ecclesiastical machinery. It provides a sense of movement while avoiding having to deal with the more difficult and fundamental aspects of theology and the faith.

From the perspective of the local church, the fewer changes in the organization the better. People look to the church as a source of stability in an unstable world. The continual changing of the organization, and particularly the nomenclature, tends to create confusion, which may be all out of proportion to the value of such changes. There is also a time lag between when changes in the structure are made and when they are learned, understood, and implemented in the local churches. In recent years it has appeared that by the time the people in the local congregations become thoroughly familiar with a new structure, a new set of changes is adopted.

As changes in the organization of the denomination and the local church are proposed, their potential impact on the life and functioning of the congregation should be carefully considered. If institutional survival becomes an increasing matter of concern, there will be more changes in the organization in an attempt to make it more effective. It is important to realize that the structure is only a method by which the gospel is proclaimed and the Christian community organized. Any structure within limits can facilitate or impede the ministry of the local church. United Methodists should consider any proposed organizational changes in the light of their impact on the effectiveness of the local congregation.

As Goes the Local Church

For The United Methodist Church, as for every other denomination, the local congregation has been and will continue to be the basic unit. It has survived and prospered in virtually every type of social and economic system. It has endured persecution, approval, and indifference by the larger society. It has had its periods of revival and times of falling away.

People discover, accept, and are nurtured in the Christian faith through their participation in the local church. The congregation is the tangible expression of Christianity in its community. For most people the Christian church is represented by a local group that meets in a specialized building and has a name such as Trinity, Epworth, First, St. Paul, or Asbury. It is within such congregations that the members find their religious experiences and participate in the ministry of the Christian church. The vitality of the entire Christian movement depends on the health and strength of the local churches. As goes the local church, so goes the denomination.

The local church, like any other social institution, will have its share of disagreements, tensions, conflicts, and other problems. It is not perfect because the people who make up its membership are not perfect. For the task of proclaiming the gospel and creating the Christian community, the local church may seem an unlikely institution. But that is what it has done for some two thousand years and that is what United Methodist congregations have done for the past two hundred. One cannot look at the local church without being profoundly aware of the powerful influence it has had on the lives of millions of people. Each time the local congregation gathers, it represents a continuing fulfillment of the statement, "And I, when I am lifted up from the earth, will draw all men to myself" (John 12:32 RSV).

Notes

Chapter 1

1. I am indebted to Dennis M. Campbell for his paper, "The Relationship of United Methodist Theology of the Church to the Structure and Organization of the Local Congregation," which was prepared as a part of this project.
2. Albert C. Outler, ed., *John Wesley* (New York: Oxford University Press, 1964), p. 312.
3. *The Book of Discipline of The United Methodist Church* (Nashville: The United Methodist Publishing House, 1976), p. 19.
4. *The Book of Worship for Church and Home* (Nashville: The United Methodist Publishing House, 1964), p. 12.

Chapter 2

1. I wish to thank Paula E. Gilbert for preparing a background paper, "Assessing the Impact of the Wesleyan Tradition upon the Structure of United Methodist Congregations."
2. Outler, pp. 91-104.
3. John Wesley, *The Letters of the Rev. John Wesley, A.M.*, ed. John Telford (London: Epworth Press, 1931), vol. 7, March 23, 1780 to July 24, 1787.

Chapter 4

1. I wish to thank William H. Willimon for contributing a background paper, "Unifying Factors for a Congregation," to this project.

Chapter 7

1. Roy H. Short, *United Methodism in Theory and Practice* (Nashville: Abingdon, 1974), p. 12.

Chapter 8

1. I am indebted to Paul A. Mickey for his paper, "Power and Authority in the Local Church: The Management of United Methodist Congregations."
2. Lyle E. Schaller, *The Multiple Staff and the Larger Church* (Nashville: Abingdon, 1980), p. 44.

Chapter 9

1. I am indebted to Lawrence E. Johnson for his paper, "The Role of Black Congregations in a Predominantly White Denomination."
2. *Ibid.*, p. 35.

Chapter 10

1. Alan K. Waltz, *Images of the Future* (Nashville: Abingdon, 1980), p. 26.
2. Rupert E. Davies, *Methodism* (Baltimore: Penguin Books, 1963), p. 12.
3. *Ibid.*